COVENANTED HAPPINESS

By the same author

Conscience and Freedom
Authority and Freedom in the Church

Covenanted Happiness

Love and commitment in marriage

Cormac Burke

IGNATIUS PRESS
SAN FRANCISCO

The typesetting of this book
was produced by
Seton Music Graphics Ltd,
Gurtycloona, Bantry, Co. Cork,
for Ignatius Press,
2515 McAllister St.,
San Francisco, CA 94118.

Nihil obstat: Stephen J. Green, *censor deputatus.*
Imprimi potest: Desmond, Archbishop of Dublin, 21 June 1990

LIBRARY OF CONGRESS CATALOG CARD NUMBER 90–82157

ISBN 0–89870–313–1

Printed in England
by Billing & Son, Worcester.

Contents

PROGRESS, LIFE AND HAPPINESS

No more than sixty years ago, contraception was rejected by Protestants as well as Catholics, as being gravely contrary to the natural order and dignity of married sexuality.[1] Forty or fifty years ago, divorce was an exceptional phenomenon, and one that carried with it a considerable social stigma. Thirty years ago, abortion was a criminal offence in all countries and in almost all cases; it was moreover something which practically no woman would contemplate.

The picture looks very different today. Contraception, divorce and abortion are approved by the legislations of almost all countries, and for millions of persons are accepted facts of modern life. If people in Western countries were asked, "Do you regard the legalization of divorce or abortion, or of the sale of contraceptives, as a mark of a progressive society?", the great majority would in all probability answer that they do.

Many people, then, are prepared today to identify these phenomena as signs of progress. But, on what do they base their opinion? Is it supported by sociological evidence? Is it the result of their having personally thought the matter out in depth? It is not at all clear that it is so.

Progress is a fine word. But progress can mean all sorts of different things. Is a society progressing because it has acquired the capacity to produce atomic weapons, or its space-craft can get to Mars or farther, or its citizens can dial Australia direct? . . . The techniques of warfare may be progressing, the speed of intercontinental or interplanetary communication may be progressing. But—is *man* progressing? That surely is the real question.

Is man progressing? As should be clear, it is not possible to answer this question without assigning a goal to man, because progress does not mean advancing in any direction (to advance in *any* direction may be actually to lose ground); it means advancing towards a goal, i.e. towards something that one positively wishes to attain, because it seems worth attaining.

Few people would object to the proposition that man's goal is happiness. What man really wants is not mainly more speed, or more efficiency, or even more money, but more happiness. Is that what he is getting nowadays? Is modern society unquestionably progressing towards greater happiness? Again, it is not all that clear.

Along with the right to life and liberty, the right to pursue happiness is a precious human right. But just as one can lose one's life or freedom, so one can lose one's happiness, or fail ever to find it—however much one pursues it. One can fail to find it because one does not look for it where it is, or does not look for it in the proper way. There are certain rules for finding happiness, and for keeping it once found; just as there are certain rules for finding and keeping one's freedom, or as there are certain rules for living itself. Life has its rules, and if they are not observed, the result can be a loss of life, or at least the failure to achieve a free or a happy life. Freedom and happiness are ours not absolutely, but conditionally; the condition is that we respect the rules of life.

Some people just *don't know* these rules, and so they break them out of ignorance. But the rules still operate, and the consequences of breaking them have to be paid. Ignorance can be very costly. An electric current can kill; so can poison: these are not just laws of physics or chemistry, they are truths about the effect of physical or chemical realities on human life. Therefore, they are truths or laws of life itself. A person may not know that a live electricity cable can kill, and so touches one; a person may not be aware that a certain chemical mixture is poisonous, and so drinks it. . . . Such persons may be quite sincere and blameless in their ignorance. But ignorance does not insulate against electricity, and sincerity is no antidote to poison. Certain actions have been performed, actions that contravene a fundamental law of life—the law of survival— and the inevitable consequences follow.

Other people *affect* an ignorance which is certainly not intelligent and can hardly be sincere. A person, for instance, may *choose* to ignore the law that demands respect for other people's property, and make off with his neighbour's wallet;

another may similarly decide to ignore the law of gravity and stop off the top of the World Trade Center, insisting that he has a *right* to a "happy" landing. . . . In these cases, the question whether ignorance is due to affectation, delusion or insincerity, can be shelved, since it will scarcely modify the definitive consequences of such persons' actions, which is that they do not find happiness. One will quite probably find prison. The other will certainly find death. One can of course call prison or death happiness. Some people do. Most people don't.

One meets other cases still: persons, for instance, who are not so much ignorant of the rules of life as *irritated* by them. They don't "see" why they have to be dictated to by life (by Nature, by God). . . . They prefer to do the dictating. They want happiness from life; they want it now, and they want it on their own terms. They are determined to live their own life, without having to heed all those complications and bends. But, does the life they live turn out to be a happy life?

Their attitude is comparable to that of an irritable motorist who suddenly wants to know why the blazes the road isn't straighter, and therefore drives on as if it actually were straight, as if the curves didn't really exist. The result of such driving is pretty obvious. So it is with the person who demands the "right" to find happiness in sex, in drink, in drugs. On they go, on *their* way to happiness. But their way does not lead to happiness. Along that way what they find is not happiness, but obsession or alcoholism or addiction, which are simply forms of slavery. Some people, again, may call slavery happiness. Most people do not.

All of these people presumably want (or wanted) happiness from life. They are not or were not wrong in wanting it. They were wrong simply in wanting it in the wrong way. They were, one might say, wrong in trying to lay down the conditions of happiness, to dictate those conditions to life itself. We cannot dictate to life as we please, certainly not in the matter of happiness. No one finds happiness on his own terms, but only on the terms on which life gives it. We cannot lay down the terms of happiness. Life itself, with its rules, lays down those terms. If one plays the game, if one accepts the terms, if one obeys the rules, one can have a reasonable hope of happiness. Not otherwise.

Now there are certain things to which all of this applies in a very special way. There are realities in life which are specially capable of giving happiness, but not to the person who attempts to bend them, at will, in any way. They are not meant to be bent that way, or to be bent that far. And if they are so bent, they break. They incidentally almost always break their benders with them. Among these realities is the relationship between man and woman, particularly as experienced both in their union in marriage as well as in the family, i.e., in the children to whom their union naturally tends.

As the title of the book is intended to suggest, the happiness that marriage can and should give is rooted in the covenantal and committed nature of married love. As Pope John Paul II says, "the covenant of conjugal love . . . is publicly affirmed as unique and exclusive, in order to live in complete fidelity to the plan of God, the Creator. A person's freedom, far from being restricted by this fidelity, is secured against every form of subjectivism or relativism and is made a sharer in creative Wisdom."[2] And a person's happiness, far from being restricted by the covenanted commitment to marriage and the family, is endowed by it with depth, maturity and permanence.

The first chapters in this book deal with factors that affect the happiness of husband and wife, in their mutual relations and their understanding and planning of married life. The commitment of husband and wife, however, is not just to one another; it is also and especially to their children. And the personal happiness of husband and wife is necessarily inter-linked with their children's happiness. Particular attention therefore has been given to the question of divorce which not only splits spouse from spouse, but also of course separates children from parents.

In two successive chapters we examine the temptation (greatly intensified in our days) of looking on divorce as the easy (the happy?) way out of married difficulties; and argue that a husband or wife, in divorcing, sacrifices far more in terms of real personal happiness—for himself or herself, as well as for the children—than he or she can ever get out of it.

The marriage covenant, with its commitment *not* to divorce, places demands on the spouses' love for one another, and especially on their love for their children. But it is a condition of real happiness for all concerned in married and family life.

Parents naturally want their children to be happy; without a well-formed *conscience*, and without true and worthwhile *ideals*, young people are not prepared for life and can never find real or lasting happiness. So we devote two further chapters to considering ways in which parents need to form their children's conscience, from early childhood; and to how, later on, they need to understand and foster their adolescent and christian ideals.

The happiness of a family can be threatened by softness or selfishness coming from within, but also and very strongly by forces from outside. If parents are committed to building the present and future happiness of their children, the permissiveness of modern society is certainly not their ally. And so we have included some considerations on how parents must help their children realize that if happiness is a prize that can be won or lost, generosity and firmness are necessary if a person is to keep his or her ideals, also in the midst of a permissive society which is largely built on the false proposition that happiness can be had on one's own terms, without self-control or generosity and basically through self-centred living.

An Appendix on the subject of abortion is included because, apart from the other moral considerations involved, abortion has probably come to be the greatest threat to the peace of mind and happiness, and the souls, of so many women and girls in today's world.

In short, we will try to analyze the reasons why married love and family life so often do not seem to give today the happiness that people surely have the right to expect from them, and what needs to be done in order to refind—or not to lose—that happiness.

1 *Marriage in Crisis?*

Marriage seems to have gone wrong for modern men and women. They seem uncertain and even disillusioned about it, as is evident from the upsurge of divorces all over the Western world. As we mentioned in our Introduction, divorce may indeed have become a mark of so-called progressive societies; but people can only regard facilities for divorce as "progressive" to the extent to which they feel that marriage is likely to break down—just as people tend to look for a moneyback warranty only insofar as they feel they are unlikely to be satisfied with the goods they have purchased. There is no getting away from the fact: a world that is beginning to believe in divorce is beginning to disbelieve in marriage.

Whatever way it is looked at, every divorce is a sign of failure. Plenty of people argue in favor of divorce. Practically no one argues that divorce is a good thing; only, at the most, that it is a lesser evil: that to get divorced is a lesser evil than to remain bound by a failed marriage.

Divorce is always a profession of failure and disillusionment. There can be few experiences more shattering to human nature than that of a couple who once felt they were made for one another, that each represented for the other the most unique and wonderful person in the world, and who now feel that they just cannot stand each other, that they cannot possibly get along together.

When all is said and done, divorce marks the final collapse for two people, and their final rejection, of an ideal and dream of happiness on which they had embarked five, ten or twenty years earlier. And that dream was the dream of a happy marriage.

Can it be "natural" for marriage to go wrong?

Marriage is obviously one of the most natural things in human society; the tendency towards marriage is obviously one of the most natural things in human nature. But if one regards marriage as something natural to man, it seems hard to suppose that in any normal state of affairs, it is natural for marriage to go wrong for him. If marriage is going wrong so often today, perhaps we are not in a normal state of affairs about marriage. Could it not be that, rather than marriage going wrong for man, it is man who has gone wrong about marriage? Is it not possible that the fault does not lie with marriage but with modern man, and specifically with his approach to marriage. I am inclined to think so, because I see at least three major points where man's approach to marriage has gone wrong:

a) his tendency to 'deify' human love; to expect from human love what any believer knows that only God can give;

b) his tendency to invert the order of priority in the *ends* or purposes of marriage, i.e. his tendency to think that marriage is primarily for the expression and enjoyment of love, and secondarily (if at all) for having children;

c) his tendency to see opposition between these two ends, instead of seeing them as complementary to one another.

Let us examine each one of these points a little more closely.

What only God can give

Man's main hope is the hope of happiness. Man is made for happiness and must necessarily seek it. But he is only going to find frustration if he looks for happiness where it is not to be found . . . ; or if he looks for unlimited happiness where only limited happiness can be found . . . ; or if he looks for happiness where it can be found, but not in the way in which it can be found there. . . .

Happiness can be found in marriage, but not unlimited happiness; to ask perfect happiness of marriage is to ask too much. Nevertheless, man is made with a capacity and thirst for unlimited happiness. And that is why it has been so well said that "woman promises to man what only God can give." Any believer knows that the perfect happiness man seeks can only be found in God. He also knows that such perfect happi-

13

ness is not possible in any real or lasting way here on earth. It can only be found in heaven. But the unbeliever, or the half-believer, forgets this. And when man begins to forget God and to lose the hope of eternal life, his heart centers on earthly things and tries to satisfy its thirst for happiness in them. It cannot. Not even in marriage which of all human things promises most happiness and should be capable of giving it. But it cannot give enough.

The person who remembers this will look for happiness in marriage, but will not look for perfect happiness, for he knows that is to look for what it cannot give. The person who forgets God will tend to "deify" human love, and to do so is to practically guarantee the failure of human love. If one expects *too much* from love and marriage, one is *bound* to be disappointed. If one puts too much pressure on a boiler, it explodes. If one asks too much of marriage, it collapses. So many modern divorces have their explanation right here.

Children as "optional extras"

The second reason why marriage often goes wrong for modern man is his tendency to create a new priority in the ends or purposes of marriage; his tendency to make the enjoyment of mutual love the main purpose, or even the whole and all-sufficient purpose, of marriage, at the same time as he reduces the possibility of children—of one or two children—to a mere factor which most couples may well want as part of their self-fulfillment, though other couples, with equal legitimacy, will perhaps prefer one or two cars or one or two homes. . . .

For many people today children are to marriage what accessories are to cars: "optional extras". Count them in if you like them or can afford them. If not, the marriage—like the car—can work perfectly well without them. To this the Church flatly says No. Only in truly exceptional cases can marriage work well without children, without the children that God wants for each individual marriage. It is of course possible that God may not want any children for a particular marriage, even though husband and wife were anxious to have a family. These (materially) sterile unions can be happy if they accept God's will. They will receive special graces from Him to learn to love one another more and more as each day passes. And they can—and indeed should—achieve a *spiritual* fruitfulness, by devoting the time and energy that would have gone to their children, to formative and apostolic activities in favor of others. But the deliberate exclusion of children, in whole or in part, is almost certain to make any marriage work badly. . . . This is a truth—a rule or law of life—which is in fact implicit in the Church's teaching about the ends of marriage and the relationship between them.

"Motives" are not always the same as "ends"

Since contemporary man has little evidence for thinking that modern philosophies of marriage are correct, he would do well to reexamine the Church's teaching—that "marriage and married love are by their nature ordered to the procreation and education of children"[1]—and her claim that this teaching represents the really natural view of marriage. It might help him if we pointed out, to begin with, that most of those who think the Church is wrong in this teaching have not properly understood what in fact the Church is teaching. The Church is not speaking about the *motives* of individuals in marrying, but about the *ends* of marriage as an institution. And a very little reflection makes it clear that subjective and personal motives do not necessarily coincide with objective ends.

The main motive most people have for marrying is undoubtedly love: "Why do I want to marry this person, rather than anyone else? Because I'm in love with him or her." That is clear. If having children enters, as a motive for marrying, it normally enters as a secondary motive, and in certain cases today it may not even enter at all.

Now, with this order of motives for marrying—first, love; secondarily (if at all), children—many people may easily conclude that a successful or happy marriage is dependent on the same factors and in the same order; i.e. that happiness in marriage depends mainly or even exclusively upon their mutual love and secondarily or not at all on having children. But there is no special evidence to show that this conclusion is correct. One thing, after all, is one's motives for marrying. And another is the *way* marriage gives happiness.

15

Understanding how marriage gives happiness

People are not wrong to marry for love. People are not wrong to hope for happiness from marriage. But people may be wrong if they stake all their hopes for happiness in marriage on just one factor—mutual love—when nature has designed married happiness to result from the delicate and exacting interplay of two factors: love and children. In other words, people may be wrong or go wrong because they have not understood how marriage is meant to work, because they have not grasped the way marriage is meant to fulfill its possibilities, including its possibility of happiness. And this is where the Church's teaching can set them right.

Only ignorance—or something worse than ignorance—could present the Church's traditional teaching on marriage as if it were the fruit of a medieval legalism; as if it were the attitude of a few diehard clerical celibates wagging a reproving finger at modern man and saying: "*You* may be interested in happiness. But that is a modern fad, and you had better forget about it if you want to remain a dutiful member of the Church; for *the Church* is not interested in whether marriage gives happiness or not. The Church's interest is simply in offspring—in numbers—and in the law: indissolubility. . . ."

The Church and human happiness

That would be a vulgar and slanderous parody of the Church's attitude. The Church is fully conscious that the truth she is upholding—in the traditional teaching about marriage—is the truth entrusted to her by Christ; and therefore that it is not in her power to alter or fail to proclaim this truth. At the same time, however, she is equally conscious that her view of marriage takes all of its natural elements into account, including that promise of happiness which it seems to offer to man. When she joins her children together in matrimony, the Church is the first to rejoice at their love and happiness. The divine Master is always a willing guest if he is invited to the marriage feast; with his presence he wishes to confirm the joy of Cana. But it is to him that a young couple must look if they want the wine of their present happiness to grow richer and

16

flow more abundantly, and never to run out or sour into vinegar.[2] When our Lord speaks to them—in Scripture, teaching that they are now one flesh and shall not be separated,[3] that they should increase and multiply;[4] or through his Church, teaching them (once again in words of Vatican II) that "the institution of marriage and married love is ordered to the procreation and education of children, and in them finds its crowning glory"[5]—he also has their happiness in mind: not only their eternal happiness (though that is what essentially matters) but also that relative but very real happiness here on earth that they can attain and he wants them to attain.

Married love is meant to become family love

Perhaps we can put it this way. It seems evidently a part of the natural order that man should see a promise of happiness in marriage. Now if, as the Church teaches, it is also part of the natural order that marriage is for having children even more than for enjoying love, then—unless nature is lying or at least inconsistent—happiness in marriage is normally and in the long run more likely to depend on having and rearing children than on mutual love between husband and wife, and its expressions. It undoubtedly depends on both factors; but the teaching of the Church would seem to suggest that, in the long run, children have a greater influence in determining the outcome of a happy marriage.

Now if someone jumps up to object that this is absurd: that it is tantamount to saying that something physiological (procreation) is more important than something spiritual (love), I would answer that it is tantamount to saying no such thing. It is to say something quite different: which is that love in marriage, which is certainly wider than mere physical love, is *wider also than mere married love*; i.e. love in marriage is not meant to remain (and is not likely to survive if it does remain) just the love of two people for each other. It is meant to broaden, to spread out, to include more. Married love is really designed to become family love. The love of husband and wife is meant to grow and, in growing, to extend to and embrace others, who will be precisely the fruit of that love. "True mutual love transcends the community of husband and

17

wife, and reaches out to its natural fruit, the children."[6] And this already brings us to the third point of our consideration.

Calculated happiness

An age that does not see children as a natural consequence of married love, may be on its way towards seeing them as its natural enemy. That is why I have suggested that a third main reason why so many marriages do not work out today is the growing modern tendency not only to put mutual love before children, but to see actual *opposition* between these two ends of marriage instead of seeing them as complementary.

Under the influence of birth control thinking and propaganda, many people today have fallen into the idea I have just been outlining: that human happiness in marriage depends essentially on love, and much less so, if at all, on paternity. I wonder how many are aware that this idea can be just the first in a series of steps by which a person may be carried forward—much farther than he had originally anticipated or wanted—by a philosophy which has its own powerful momentum and direction.

Let us analyze a little deeper this first step in the birth control philosophy, and see how it easily leads people on—down a path of calculation, rather than up one of love.

The first principle of this modern "philosophy" of marriage, then, is that love is the essential and all-sufficient constituent of married happiness, and children, therefore, are to be regarded as a possible help—but also as a possible hindrance—to that love. For children make demands, and there is being popularized today a concept of love that does not want to have demands made of it. With this mentality, when love is thought of above all in terms of personal satisfaction (and not of *rising* towards an ideal, or of *self-giving*, with all this implies of struggle and *sacrifice*), then a vague hankering after paternity may not be enough to outweigh the "disadvantages" of children. This is becoming especially true in the case of women among whom there is a growing tendency to feel that the burdens of pregnancy and child-rearing are just too high a price to pay for the possible satisfactions that may derive from them.

18

Happiness is the result of a generous dedication to someone or something worthwhile. It is the result of giving oneself without counting the cost. Happiness is not something that can be purchased for money, or obtained through calculation. Yet the whole of this modern philosophy of marriage is becoming replete with calculations, practically all of them cold, and many of them quite selfish and quite mistaken.

The first calculation is—as we have seen—that two people suffice to make each other happy. The second calculation is that a certain number of children—one or two—may be a help to that happiness; or may equally be a hindrance. . . . The third calculation—which is beginning to have the force of a dogma for many today—is that *more than a certain number* of children (two or three at a maximum) will *certainly* run counter to married love and happiness. Now, evidently, once one concludes that a particular number of children—four, for instance—is bound to be inimical to love, one can easily end up regarding *any* number—even one—as an enemy. This is simply the logic of birth control marriage.

Once two people have begun to believe that they are "made for one another", they may end up believing that they are not made for anyone else, and have no need for anyone else; that anyone else—even their child, and even *especially* their child—may be a rival to their love. One or other, or both, may anticipate—and refuse to accept—the possibility of the child's absorbing part of the love which their partner has hitherto given exclusively to them. It is of course a fact that most husbands and wives, on becoming parents, feel some reactions of jealousy at sensing themselves no longer the exclusive object of their partner's affections. It is natural to experience some passing motions of jealousy in this sense, just as it is natural to overcome them. What is not natural, when one has anticipated this new possible polarization or broadening out of one's partner's love, is to want to avoid having the child that will cause it. This is simply possessiveness and selfish grasping: the very antithesis of love.

Sexual love and procreation are joined in God's plans, to form a strong natural support for marriage and happiness. Man can certainly set apart what God has joined together. But

19

this unnatural separation may leave married love without support. And marriage without its natural support logically collapses.

Those who believe that the birth control philosophy favors marriage and love would do well therefore to look to its possible ultimate consequences. These have been well parodied in Aldous Huxley's *Brave New World*, that satire of a soulless future society which now looks much less impossible than when Huxley conceived it fifty years ago. That brave and liberated vision of planned things to come—love and sex identified (or rather, love smothered and lost in uncontrolled animal instinct); marriage excluded and abolished: children (repopulating) reduced to laboratory processes, in the safe and exclusive hands of the State—is just the fantastic (but ultimate) projection of the birth control philosophy.

Opposition between the ends?

When the Church teaches that "married love is ordered to procreation"[7] it would be a crass error to interpret this sub-ordering of love to procreation as if it implied a slighting attitude on the Church's part towards love. The Church is not opposing one end of marriage to another. It is modern man who is doing that. The Church sees the intimate harmony between all the natural aspects of marriage—its objective purposes as well as its subjective motives.[8] To indicate that one thing is ordained to another is to *give the key to its true nature*. And so the Church, in teaching that mutual love in marriage is subordinate to procreation, far from slighting human love, is giving us the key to nature's plan for the fulfillment, within marriage, of the great expectations of human love.

Love's greatest project—children

Nature has designed married love to be fruitful.[9] Fruitfulness, in other words, is natural to love. It is something that love naturally longs for, so much so that love feels frustrated if it cannot bear fruit.

Love always inspires; it dreams of great things even when it is unrequited. Requited love—love that has been answered by love—no longer just dreams of great things; it yearns with the ambition, and feels the strength, to carry them out.

Love enables a young couple to find a thrill of happiness in situations where those not in love experience no more than boredom and routine. To thrill them, it is enough that they can do or choose something—almost anything—together, and that what they do or choose represents the fruit of a loving decision: the meeting point of two wills in love. As they await their wedding day, an engaged couple work happily on so many projects—minor and even trivial projects, in themselves—that will help to make up their new life together. They enthusiastically plan and choose the apartment they are going to live in, the type of furniture they will have, the very color of carpets or curtains. . . .

Is it possible, then, for them not to thrill together with enthusiasm at the major project that nature has reserved for them, a project that will be uniquely theirs and exclusive to their union; a project that will be no mere choice of something material—like a car or a hi-fi—but a genuine *creation* on their part (with God's collaboration) of living beings, their own children . . . ? Other couples may live in houses identical to theirs, or may choose the same model car or television set, or much more expensive ones. . . . No one but they can have *their* children.

How could a couple not look on the project of their children as the greatest and most precious of all their projects, since they can see that it alone—among them all—is the direct fruit of their most intimate married union, fruit of the union not only of their wills but also of their bodies? And as they reflect on all of this, is it possible that they should fail to understand the greatness and sacredness of God's plan for marriage?

That is why a young couple in love—if they understand love as meaning something more than the mere gratification of instinct—are not satisfied with a barren union. If children are the natural fruit of married love, the married love that does not bear that fruit—when it can do so—frustrates itself and may soon wither and die. Its danger is self-suffocation, for it must try to survive in a closed and unnatural atmosphere where it has deprived itself of the breath of life.

21

If nature has designed married love to be fruitful, we can say that it has also designed that growth in love will normally be in function of growth in fruitfulness. The couple that expects their love to grow while at the same time they neglect or frustrate its fruitfulness, are denaturalizing their marriage. They have not understood the way that marriage can normally give happiness, and are not likely to find the happiness that their marriage could have given them. Their love, without the protection and strength it is meant to draw from children, can easily give way before the pressures of life.

Every marriage passes through a crisis

I do not think it is hard to follow nature's plan which has designed children to be not only the fruit but also the safeguard of mutual love between the spouses, and the mainstay of their married happiness.

Each marriage comes to a critical period, a turning point towards a fuller and more definitive good, or towards bad. That moment can come quite early on—as soon as easy romance fades, which may often be no more than a couple of years after marriage. If a couple does not negotiate that critical moment properly, their marriage will begin to go downhill. Mutual understanding and respect will lessen; rows will become more frequent. They will have begun the gradual process of drifting apart that can end in final estrangement ten or fifteen years later.

A double need

I would say that a double need must be satisfied if a marriage is to survive this period of crisis. When that testing time arrives, each spouse needs, in the first place, a major motive to help them to be *loyal* to the other person despite his or her defects, a motive sufficient to keep them working at the task of *learning to love* the other person.

And each one needs, in the second place, a powerful motive to improve personally: to become a less self-centered, a more lovable person. It is easy to see in children nature's special way of providing both motives.

Let us consider the first point: the need to keep loving when love begins to be hard. In heaven, God and the saints love without effort. But earth is not heaven. Love on earth is seldom easy; and if it is easy for a time, the easiness does not tend to last. It is true that there must indeed be a great depth of goodness in each human person, for God loves each of us with an immense love, and God only loves what is good. But we are not God, and at times we find it hard to discover the good points in other people. In fact we often seem to have a greater facility for seeing people's defects than their virtues. This specially happens when two people share life as closely and constantly as in marriage. And it happens above all if, in their shared life, *they have remained alone*. Two people constantly face to face are going to see far more defects in each other than two people who are looking together at their children.

When little difficulties in getting on begin to crop up, the thought of their children—if there are children—should easily and naturally enter as a main motive in determining husband or wife to be faithful to their marriage vows. "For better or for worse", they promised years ago. . . . It will clearly be worse, for the children, if their parents don't learn to get along. "For richer or for poorer" . . . ; the children will clearly be poorer if they live in a disunited or a broken home. Can any stronger motives exist for a couple—than the responsibility and love they have towards their children—to push and encourage and compel them to be faithful, whatever the cost, whatever their feelings, whatever the state of their nerves, whatever efforts—however extraordinary—they may have to make? It may certainly be tough on them to make those efforts, but a moment's reflection should tell them that if they are not prepared to make them, it is going to be much tougher on their children.

There is the first motive, and nature's way of supplying it. "For our children's sake, we must learn to get along. And therefore I will fight with all my strength to keep loving my partner. And, with God's grace, I will succeed."

The husband or wife who reacts so is already improving as a person. And this brings us directly to the second point. If love is to survive in marriage each spouse must learn to love the other, with his or her defects. But if love is not just to survive, but to grow, then each spouse must be able to discover virtues—new virtues or increased virtues—in the other.

If love is to grow in marriage, the other person must appear as more and more lovable. And he (or she) will not, unless he is improving, unless he is actually turning into a better person.

On the natural level, generosity and self-giving are what make a person better and more lovable. And it is selfishness that kills love both in the selfish person himself as well as in those who have contact with him or her.

The person in love needs to be able to sacrifice himself for the loved one, *if he himself is to become more lovable*. The person incapable of sacrifice is incapable of giving or receiving (or retaining) much love.

It is good that each spouse sacrifices himself for the other. But it is doubtful, on a natural level, if any husband or wife can, alone, inspire their partner indefinitely to generosity and self-sacrifice.

We have said that the person in love needs to be able to sacrifice himself for the loved one, if he himself is to become more lovable. We should add that *the loved one*, in Nature's plan for marriage, *includes children*. Children can and do draw from parents a degree of sacrifice to which neither parent, alone, could probably inspire the other. "A man most easily rises above himself for the sake of his children. Parental love is the most naturally disinterested kind of love."[10] In this way, as they sacrifice themselves for their children, each parent actually improves and becomes—in their partner's eyes also—truly a more lovable person. "For the sake of their children, spouses rise above themselves, and above a limited view of their own happiness. Moral stature is only acquired if one rises above oneself. Children, above all, are what spur a couple on to a moral greatness."[11]

Marriage has need of sacrifice

On the other hand, if a couple leave untapped the capacity for sacrifice stored in their paternal or maternal instincts, they are likely to end up, at best, as half-developed person, half-lovable persons. And that may not be good enough for the survival of their marriage.

The fact is that sacrifice is a positive need for married life. In particular all the sacrifice that children demand of their parents from their earliest years is a major factor designed by nature to mature and develop and unite the parents. It is good that the husband and wife sacrifice themselves for each other. But it is even better that both together make sacrifices for their children. Shared sacrifice is one of the best bonds of love.

When love is left without support . . .

It seems to me that one of the most obvious, frequent and saddest mistakes of many young couples today embarking on marriage is the decision to postpone having any children for a number of years—two or three or five—after getting married. The result is that *precisely in that moment* when romance starts to fade, when their love begins to run into difficulties and *needs support*, the main support which nature had thought of (had "planned", I would say) for that moment—their children—*does not exist*.

Shared selfishness is no basis for happiness

I know that many young couples want to enjoy themselves for a number of years. They feel too young for settling down to family life, and prefer to combine what they consider the advantages of married life with the continued attractions of the social life to which they have become accustomed. Can this be seriously regarded as a *natural* approach to marriage? Does it not look too much to what marriage offers in the way of enjoyment and too little to what it implies in the way of commitment? May there not be as much of shared selfishness as of shared love in such an approach? When all is said and done, "to have a good time together" is not much of an ideal for two people to share, and is certainly not capable of holding them together, in love, for a lifetime.

At times one gets the impression today that many young couples are planning for a marriage where the need for sacrifice will be reduced to a minimum and, if possible, absolutely eliminated. The saddest thing about this is that a couple who want a marriage without sacrifice, want a marriage where they will eventually lose respect for one another.

When is one mature enough to start a family

Others argue that a few years of married life together will help them mature more and so be better prepared for starting and rearing a family. But what, it may be asked, is there in such a shared life together—with its minimum of burdens—that is really maturing them? The moment when a couple is best prepared for starting a family is the moment when they have just got married. The romance that still accompanies those early years of married life will help them face up more readily and cheerfully to the sacrifices that children demand. This romantic and more idealistic love is actually designed by nature to facilitate the process by which a couple matures in sacrifice. Later on, it will not be so easy and may not work. If they leave having their first children for later on—when romantic love perhaps no longer accompanies them—the dedication and sacrifice children require may prove too much—precisely because they have not matured enough.

If two young people in love don't want to start a family, they would be wise not to try to start a marriage. It's too likely to fail. One might compare it to starting a car, while leaving its generator belt somehow stuck and motionless. The car may run all right for a while, but in the end its motor is bound to seize up. . . .

The most experienced family planner

It would be a funny world if nature were not in fact the best and wisest Family Planner. She is certainly the Planner with the longest experience. The results of modern—artificial and

26

anti-natural—family planning are beginning to be abundantly clear: more and more crumbling marriages, more and more broken homes, more and more isolated people. . . . Those young couples who are tempted to trust the demographers or the politicians or the sociologists, rather than nature; those who are tempted to bend to social pressures or to the simple desire for an easy life rather than heed their instincts of paternity, would do well to ask themselves if they really believe—on the evidence—that modern family planning seems to be making for happier marriages, or whether the plan of nature is not more farseeing and more likely to provide the support for a strong and lasting married life and married love.

Self-enrichment in marriage

Those who maintain that the main purpose of marriage is the enrichment of the spouses' personalities, their self-fulfillment as they complement one another through their mutual love, should also be prepared to say what in fact personal fulfillment implies. Their meaning, presumably, is that marriage is meant to make a fuller human person of each spouse: to make a fuller man or a fuller woman, of husband or wife. But it would help if they went on to say in what this fuller humanity consists: in a greater capacity of understanding? a greater spirit of sacrifice or self-giving? a more developed self-control? . . . Or (I am assuming that they would not maintain that is consists in a greater dependence on physical sex) would they suggest that it consists in a greater concern precisely with self, accompanied by a growing indifference towards others? . . .

Pope Paul's words are worth reflecting on. A married love that is fully *human*, he insists, is "a compound of sense and spirit. It is not, then, merely a question of natural instinct or emotional drive. It is also, and above all, an act of the free will, whose dynamism ensures that not only does it endure through the joys and sorrows of daily life, but also that it grows, so that husband and wife become in a way one heart and one soul, and together attain their human fulfillment." [12]

Dictatorial pressures

We would return to the suggestion with which we began: that it is not marriage that has gone wrong for modern man, it is modern man who has gone wrong about marriage. He has abused it, and it no longer works in his service.

For too long some people have been crying, "We have the right to be happy in marriage without being dictated to by the Church." One begins to note a hollow tone of despair in the cry, for the very people who pay least heed to the laws of the Church are those who are finding least happiness in marriage.

There is dictation today—and dictatorial pressure—about marriage. But it is not coming from the Church. It is coming from the State, from the social planners, from the economic experts, or from the philosophers of a pervasive hedonism or an aimless libertarianism.

It is no wonder if these man-imposed plans for marriage end in failure, for marriage is not man's idea, but God's; and it can only work—and give happiness—if it is lived according to God's plans.

People have indeed the right to expect happiness from marriage, but only from the type of marriage that nature instituted, and only when it is lived, with God's grace, in accordance with its natural design and its natural laws. Not to respect that design or those laws is to denaturalize what was made to help man towards his happiness and salvation, and to turn it—sooner or later—into a source of his misery and frustration.

Marriage is in crisis, and seems to be in decline in many modern societies. Nevertheless, one meets with so many exceptions, so many cases of happy homes, because the parents have not frustrated the noble instincts of parenthood that nature has given them. They have, on the contrary, fulfilled those instincts, and fulfilled them generously, in the conviction that "a truly noble married love aspires, with a courageous heart, to the glory of fruitfulness. But there is no glory in a strained and calculated fruitfulness. Glory lies in an abundant fruitfulness, in the longing for that abundance. If it feels the need for reasons, it is not in order to have children, but in order to limit their number."[13]

28

The number is constantly growing of married couples who have understood the greatness of the divine plan in which God, by calling them to marriage, has given them a share. And so, strengthened by grace, they have been able to face up to the sacrifices—sacrifices of love—that love itself needs for its very survival.

2   *Married love and contraception*

There is a modern argument for conjugal contraception which claims to speak in personalist terms, and which could be summarized as follows. The marriage act has two functions: a biological or procreative function, and a spiritual-unitive function. However, while it is only potentially a procreative act, it is actually and in itself a love act: it truly expresses conjugal love and unites husband and wife. Now, while contraception frustrates the biological or procreative potential of the marital act, it fully respects its spiritual and unitive function; in fact it facilitates it by removing tensions or fears capable of impairing the expression of love in married intercourse. In other words—this position claims—while contraception suspends or nullifies the procreative aspect of marital intercourse, it leaves its unitive aspect intact.

Until quite recently, the traditional argument against artificial birth-control has mainly been that the sexual act is naturally designed for procreation, and it is wrong to frustrate this design because it is wrong to interfere with man's natural functions. Many persons do not find this traditional argument altogether convincing, and it certainly seems open to rather elementary objections. After all, we do interfere with other natural functions, for instance when we use ear-plugs or hold our nose, etc., and no one has ever argued that to do so is morally wrong. Why then should it be wrong to interfere for good reasons with the procreational aspect of marital intercourse? In any case, the defenders of contraception dismiss this traditional argument as mere "biologism"; as an understanding of the marital act that fails to go beyond its biological function or possible biological consequences, and ignores its spiritual function, i.e., its function in signifying and effecting the union of the spouses.

Those who advance this defence of marital contraception—couched in apparently personalist terms—feel they are on strong and positive ground. If we are to offer an effective answer to it and show its radical defectiveness, I would suggest that we too need to develop a personalist argument, based on a true personalist understanding of sex and marriage.

This contraceptive argument is evidently built on an essential thesis: that the procreative and the unitive aspects of the marital act are *separable*, i.e., that the procreative aspect can be nullified without this in any way vitiating the conjugal act or making it less a unique expression of true marital love and union.

This thesis is of course explicitly rejected by the Church. The main reason why contraception is unacceptable to a Christian conscience is, as Pope Paul VI put it in *Humanae Vitae*, the "*inseparable* connection, established by God . . . between the unitive significance and the procreative significance which are both inherent to the marriage act".

Paul VI affirmed this inseparable connection. He did not however go on to explain *why* these two aspects of the marital act are in fact so inseparably connected, or why this connection is such that it is the very ground of the moral evaluation of the act. Perhaps serene reflection, matured by the ongoing debate of more than twenty years, can enable us to discover the reasons why this is so: why the connection between the two aspects of the act is in fact such that the destruction of its procreative reference necessarily destroys its unitive and personalist significance. In other words, if one deliberately destroys the power of the conjugal act to give life, one necessarily destroys its power to signify love: the love and union proper to marriage.

The marital act as an act of union

Why is the act of intercourse regarded as *the* act of selfgiving, the most distinctive expression of marital love? Why is this act—which is but a passing and fleeting thing—particularly regarded as an act of *union*? After all, people in love express their love and desire to be united in many ways: sending letters, exchanging looks or presents, holding hands. . . . What makes the sexual act unique? Why does this act unite the spouses in a way that no other act does? What is it that makes it not just a physical experience but a *love* experience?

31

The special pleasure attaching to it? Is the unitive meaning of the conjugal act contained just in the sensation, however intense, that it can produce? If intercourse unites two people simply because it gives special pleasure, then it would seem that one or other of the spouses could at times find a more meaningful union outside marriage than within it. It would follow too that sex without pleasure becomes meaningless, and that sex with pleasure, even homosexual sex, becomes meaningful.

No. The conjugal act may or may not be accompanied by pleasure; but the meaning of the act does not consist in its pleasure. The pleasure provided by marital intercourse may be intense, but it is transient. The *significance* of marital intercourse is also intense, and it is not transient; it lasts.

Why should the marital act be more significant than any other expression of affection between the spouses? Why should it be a more intense expression of love and union? Surely because of *what happens* in that marital encounter, which is not just a touch, not a mere sensation, however intense, but a *communication*, an offer and acceptance, an exchange of something that uniquely represents the gift of oneself and the union of two selves.

Here of course it should not be forgotten that while two persons in love want to give themselves to one another, to be united to one another, this desire of theirs remains humanly speaking[1] on a purely volitional level. They can *bind* themselves to one another, but they cannot actually *give* themselves. The greatest expression of a person's desire to give *himself* is to give the seed of himself.[2] Giving one's seed is much more significant, and in particular is much more real, than giving one's heart. "I am yours, I give you my heart; here, take it," remains mere poetry, to which no physical gesture can give true body. But, "I am yours; I give you my seed; here, take it," is not poetry, it is love. It is conjugal love embodied in a unique and privileged physical action whereby intimacy is expressed—"I give you what I give no one"—and union is achieved: "Take what I have to give. This will be a new me. United to you, to what you have to give—to your seed—this will be a new '*you-and-me*', fruit of our mutual knowledge and love." In human terms this is the closest one can get to giving one's self conjugally and to accepting the conjugal self-gift of another, and so achieving spousal union.

Therefore, what makes marital intercourse express a *unique* relationship and union is not the sharing of a sensation but the sharing of a *power*: of an extraordinary life-related, creative physical sexual power. In a true conjugal relationship, each spouse says to the other: "I accept you as somebody like no one else in my life. You will be unique to me and I to you. You and you alone will be my husband; you alone will be my wife. And the proof of your uniqueness to me is the fact that with you—and with you alone—am I prepared to share this God-given life-oriented power."

In this consists the singular character of intercourse. Other physical expressions of affection do not go beyond the level of a mere gesture; they remain a symbol of the union desired. But the conjugal act is not a mere symbol. In true marital intercourse, something *real* has been exchanged, with a full gift and acceptance of conjugal masculinity and femininity. And there remains, as witness to their conjugal relationship and the intimacy of their conjugal union, the husband's seed in the wife's body.[3]

Now if one deliberately nullifies the life-orientation of the conjugal act, *one destroys its essential power to signify union.* Contraception in fact turns the marital act *into self-deception or into a lie*: "I love you so much that with you, and with you alone, I am ready to share this most unique power. . . ." But—*what* unique power? In contraceptive sex, no unique power is being shared, except a power to produce pleasure. But then the uniqueness of the marital act is reduced to pleasure. Its significance is gone.

Contraceptive intercourse is an exercise in meaninglessness. It could perhaps be compared to going through the actions of singing without letting any sound of music pass one's lips.

Some of us can remember the love-duets of Jeanette McDonald and Nelson Eddy, two popular singing stars of the early "talkies". How absurd if they had sung *silent* duets: going through the motions of singing, but not allowing their vocal chords to produce an intelligible sound: just meaningless reverberations . . . ; a hurry or a flurry of movement signifying nothing. Contraceptive intercourse is very much like that. Contraceptive spouses involve each other in bodily movements, but their "body language" is not truly human.[4] They refuse to let their bodies communicate sexually and intelligibly with one another. They go through the motions of a love-song; but there is no *song*.

Contraception is in fact not just an action without meaning; it is an action that contradicts the essential meaning which true conjugal intercourse should have as signifying total and unconditional self-donation.[5] Instead of accepting each other totally, contraceptive spouses reject part of each other, because fertility is part of each one of them. They reject part of their mutual love; its power to be fruitful. . . .

A couple may say: we do not want our love to be fruitful. But if that is so, there is an inherent contradiction in their trying to express their love by means of an act which, *of its nature, implies fruitful love*; and there is even more of a contradiction if, when they engage in the act, they deliberately destroy the fertility-orientation from which precisely derives its capacity to express the uniqueness of their love.

In true marital union, husband and wife are meant to experience the vibration of human vitality in its very source.[6] In the case of contraceptive "union", the spouses experience sensation, but it is drained of real vitality.

The anti-life effect of contraception does not stop at the "No" which it addresses to the possible fruit of love. It tends to take the very life out of love itself. Within the hard logic of contraception, anti-life becomes anti-love. Its devitalizing effect devastates love, threatening it with early ageing and premature death.

At this point it is good to anticipate the possible criticism that our argument so far is based on an incomplete disjunction, inasmuch as it seems to affirm that the conjugal act is either procreative or else merely hedonistic. . . . Can contraceptive spouses not counter this with the sincere affirmation that, in their intercourse, they are not merely seeking pleasure; they are also experiencing and expressing love for one another?

Let us clarify our position on this particular point. We are not affirming that contraceptive spouses may not love each other in their intercourse, nor—insofar as they are not prepared to have such intercourse with a third person—that it does not express a *certain* uniqueness in their relationship. Our thesis is that it does not express *conjugal* uniqueness. Love may somehow be present in their contraceptive relationship; conjugal love is not expressed by it. Conjugal love may in fact soon find itself threatened by it. Contraceptive spouses are constantly haunted by the suspicion that the act in which they share could indeed be, for each one of them, a privileged *giving* of pleasure, but could also be a mere selfish *taking* of pleasure. It is logical that their love-making be troubled by a sense of falseness or hollowness, for they are attempting to found the uniqueness of the spousal relationship on an act of pleasure that tends ultimately to close each one of them sterilely in on himself or herself, and they are refusing to found that relationship on the truly unique conjugal dimension of loving co-creativity capable, in its vitality, of opening each of them out not merely to one another but to the whole of life and creation.

Sexual love and sexual knowledge

The mutual and exclusive self-donation of the marriage act consists in its being the gift and acceptance of something unique. Now this something unique is not *just* the seed (this indeed could be "biologism"), but the *fullness of the sexuality* of each spouse.

It was in the context of its not being good for man to be alone that God made him sexual. He created man in a duality—male and female—with the potential to become a trinity. The differences between the sexes speak therefore of a divine plan of complementarity, of self-completion and self-fulfillment, also through self-perpetuation.

It is not good for man to be alone because man, on his own, cannot fulfill himself; he needs others. He especially needs another: a companion, a spouse. Union with a spouse, giving oneself to a spouse—sexual and marital union in self-donation— are normally a condition of human growth and fulfillment.

Marriage, then, is a means of fulfillment through union. Husband and wife are united in mutual knowledge and love, a love which is not just spiritual but also bodily; and a knowledge underpinning their love which is likewise not mere speculative or intellectual knowledge; it is bodily knowledge as well. Their marital love is also meant to be based on *carnal* knowledge; this is fully human and fully logical. How significant it is that the Bible, in the original Hebrew, refers to marital intercourse in terms of man and woman "knowing" each other. Adam, Genesis says, *knew* Eve, his wife. What comment can we make on this equivalence which the Bible draws between conjugal intercourse and mutual knowledge?

What is the distinctive knowledge that husband and wife communicate to one another? It is the knowledge of each other's integral human condition as spouse, Each "discloses" a most intimate secret to the other: the secret of his or her personal sexuality. Each is revealed to the other truly as spouse and comes to know the other in the uniqueness of that spousal self-revelation and self-gift. Each one lets himself or herself be known by the other, and surrenders to the other, precisely as husband or wife.

Nothing can undermine a marriage so much as the refusal to fully know and accept one's spouse or to let oneself be fully known by him or her. Marriage is constantly endangered by the possibility of one spouse holding something back from the other; keeping some knowledge to oneself that he or she does not want the other to possess.[7] This can occur on all levels of interpersonal communication: physical as well as spiritual.

In many modern marriages, there *is* something in the spouses, and between the spouses, that each does not want to know, does not want to face up to, wants to avoid: and this something is their sexuality. As a result, since they will not allow each other full mutual carnal knowledge, they *do not truly know each other* sexually or humanly or spousally. This places their married love under a tremendous existential tension that can tear it apart.

In true marital intercourse each spouse renounces protective self-possession, so as to *fully possess* and be *fully possessed* by the other. This fullness of true sexual gift and possession is only achieved in marital intercourse open to life. Only in procreative intercourse do the spouses exchange true "knowledge" of one another, do they truly speak humanly and intelligibly to one another; do they truly *reveal* themselves to one another in their full human actuality and potential. Each offers, and each accepts, full spousal knowledge of the other.

In the body language of intercourse, each spouse utters a word of love that is both a "self-expression"—an image of each one's self—as well as an expression of his or her longing for the other. These two words of love meet, and are fused in one. And, as this new unified word of love takes on flesh, God shapes it into a person—the child: the incarnation of the husband's and wife's sexual knowledge of one another and sexual love for one another.

In contraception, the spouses will not let the word—which their sexuality longs to utter—take flesh. They will not even truly speak the word to each other. They remain humanly impotent in the face of love; sexually dumb and carnally speechless before one another.

Sexual love is a love of the whole male or female person, body and spirit. Love is falsified if body and spirit do not say the same thing. This happens in contraception. The bodily act speaks of a presence of love or of a degree of love that is denied by the spirit. The body says, "I love you totally", whereas the spirit says, "I love you reservedly." The body says, "I seek you"; the spirit says, "I will not accept you, not all of you."

Contraceptive intercourse falls below mere pantomime. It is disfigured body-language; it expressed a rejection of the other. By it, each says: "I do not want to know you as my husband or my wife; I am not prepared to recognize you as my spouse. I want something from you, but *not* your sexuality; and if I have something to give to you, something I will let you take, it is *not* my sexuality."[8]

This enables us to develop a point we touched on a few pages back. The negation that a contraceptive couple are involved in is not directed just towards children, or just towards life, or just towards the world. They address a negation directly towards one another. "I prefer a sterile you", is equivalent to saying, "I don't want all you offer me. I have calculated the measure of my love, and it is not big enough for that; it is not able to take all of you. I want a 'you' cut down to the size of my love . . . ." The fact that both spouses may concur in accepting a cut-rate version of each other does not save their love or their lives—or their possibilities of happiness—from the effects of such radical human and sexual devaluation.

Normal conjugal intercourse fully asserts masculinity and femininity. The man asserts himself as man and husband, and the woman equally asserts herself as woman and wife. In contraceptive intercourse, only a maimed sexuality is asserted. In the truest sense sexuality is not asserted at all. Contraception represents such a refusal to let oneself be known that it simply is not real carnal knowledge. A deep human truth underlies the theological and juridical principle that contraceptive sex does not consummate marriage.

Contraceptive intercourse, then, is not real sexual intercourse at all. That is why the disjunctives offered by this whole matter are insufficiently expressed by saying that if intercourse is contraceptive, then it is merely hedonistic. This may or may not be true. What is true—at a much deeper level—is that if intercourse is contraceptive, then *it is not sexual*. In contraception there is an "intercourse" of sensation, but no real sexual knowledge or sexual love, no true sexual revelation of self or sexual communication of self or sexual gift of self. The choice of contraception is in fact the rejection of sexuality. The warping of the sexual instinct from which modern society seems to suffer represents not so much an excess of sex, as a lack of true human sexuality.

True conjugal intercourse unites. Contraception separates, and the separation works right along the line. It not only separates sex from procreation, it also separates sex from love. It separates pleasure from meaning, and body from mind. Ultimately and surely, it separates wife from husband and husband from wife.

Contraceptive couples who stop to reflect realize that their marriage is troubled by some deep malaise. The alienations they are experiencing are a sign as well as a consequence of the grave violation of the moral order involved in contraception. Only a resolute effort to break with contraceptive practices can heal the sickness affecting their married life.

This is why the teaching of *Humanae Vitae* as well as sub-sequent papal magisterium on the matter, far from being a blind adherence to an outdated posture, represent a totally clear-sighted defence of the innate dignity and true meaning of human and spousal sexuality.

Why does only procreative sex fulfill?

Our argument so far is that contraceptive marital sex does not achieve any true personalist end. It does not bring about self-fulfillment in marriage, but rather prevents and frustrates it. But—one may still ask—does it follow that procreative marital sex alone leads to the self-fulfillment of the spouses? I think it does, and that the reason lies in the very nature of love. Love is creative. God's love (if we may put it this way) "drove" him to create. Man's love, made in the image of God's, is also meant to create. If it deliberately does not do so, it frustrates itself. Love between two persons makes them want to do things together. While this is true of friendship in general, it has a singular application to the love between spouses. A couple truly in love want to do things together; if possible, they want to do something "original" together. As we saw in the last chapter, nothing is more original to a couple in love than their child: the image and fruit of their love and their union. That is why *"the* marital thing" is to have children; and other things, as substitutes, do not satisfy conjugal love.

Procreative intercourse fulfills also because only in such intercourse are the spouses open to all the possibilities of their mutual love: ready to be enriched and fulfilled not only by what it offers to them, but also by what it *demands* of them.

Further, procreative intercourse fulfills because it expresses the human person's desire for self-perpetuation. It expresses it and does not contradict it, as contraception does. It is only on life-wishes, not on death-wishes, that love can thrive. When a normal married couple have a child, they pass their child joyfully to each other. If their child dies, there is no joy, there are tears, as they pass the dead body to one another. Spouses should weep over a contraceptive act: a barren, desolate act which rejects the life that is meant to keep love alive, and would kill the life their love naturally seeks to give

39

origin to. There may be physical satisfaction, but there can be no joy in passing dead seed; or in passing living seed only to kill it.

The vitality of sensation in sexual intercourse should correspond to a vitality of meaning (remembering—as we have said—that sensation is not meaning). The very explosiveness of sexual pleasure suggests the greatness of the creativity of sex. In each conjugal act, there should be something of the magnificence—of the scope and power—of Michelangelo's Creation in the Sistine Chapel in Rome. . . . But it is the dynamism not just of a sensation, but of an event: of something that happens, of a communication of life.

A lack of true sexual awareness characterizes the act if the intensity of the pleasure does not serve to stir a fully conscious understanding of the greatness of the conjugal experience: I am committing myself—my creative life-giving power—not just to another person, but to the whole of creation: to history, to mankind, to the purposes and design of God. In each act of conjugal union, teaches Pope John Paul II, "there is renewed, in a way, the mystery of creation in all its original depth and vital power."[9]

A last point should be made. The whole question we are considering is of course tremendously complicated precisely by the strength of the sexual instinct. Nevertheless, the very strength of this instinct should itself be a pointer towards an adequate understanding of sexuality. Elementary common sense says that the power of the sexual urge must correspond to deep human aspirations or needs. It has of course been traditional to explain the sexual urge in cosmic or demographic terms: just as we have a food appetite to maintain the life of the individual, so we have a sex appetite to maintain the life of the species. This explanation makes sense—as far as it goes. However, it clearly does not go far enough. The sex appetite—the strength of the sex appetite—surely corresponds not only to cosmic or collectivist needs, but also to personalist needs. If man and woman feel a deep longing for sexual union, it is also because they have—each one personally has—a deep longing for all that is involved in true sexuality: self-giving, self-complementarity, self-realization, self-perpetuation, in spousal union with another.

The experience of such complete spousal sexuality is filled with many-facetted pleasure, in which the simple physical satisfaction of a mere sense instinct is accompanied and enriched by the personalist satisfaction of the much deeper and stronger longings involved in sex, and not marred and soured by their frustration. If continuous and growing sexual frustration is in fact a main consequence of contraception, this is also because the contraceptive mentality deprives the very power of the sexual urge of its real meaning and purpose, and then tries to find full sexual experience and satisfaction in what is basically little more than a physical release.

3 *Children as values*

A large part of my time is unfortunately spent dealing with marriage annulment cases. A frequent grounds of annulment is that consent was vitiated through the exclusion of one of the three traditional "bona" or *values* of marriage: the "bonum fidei" (fidelity to one partner; the uniqueness of the marital union), the "bonum sacramenti" (permanence of the marriage bond; the indissolubility of the union), or the "bonum prolis" (offspring; the fruitfulness of the union).

Given the aspect of *obligation* involved in each of these "bona" or values, it is logical and, I suppose, healthy enough that ecclesiastical judges like myself center their attention on the question of whether or not this obligation has been truly accepted by the person marrying. I do not think it is so healthy, however, if other people begin thinking of these "bona" mainly or simply in terms of their obligatoriness . . . . If their thinking were to go this way, they could easily come to conclude that— since an obligation is normally something burdensome, and we all tend to avoid burdens—the exclusion of permanence or fidelity or offspring cannot really be thought of as strange or exceptional; one can even begin to find good reasons for maintaining that it is something to be expected. . . .

These are of course not merely theoretical considerations. I am afraid that to quite a number of Christians today—and not least to many who have a special mission to form and guide others (pastors, teachers, counsellors . . .)—the idea of people excluding one or other of these "bona" when they marry, no longer tends to seem surprising; it even seems natural enough.

Exclusion is not natural

Exclusion, however, *is* surprising, precisely because it is *not* natural. It is not natural because one does not logically reject the obligations or responsibilities that necessarily accompany the acquisition of a GOOD thing. If the thing is good enough, the goodness more than compensates the responsibilities. The purchase of an automobile involves burdens and responsibilities; but most people regard a car as a good thing and think that, despite the burdens involved, they are enriched by the acquisition of one car, or of two or three cars, if they can afford them.[1]

Thank God for St Augustine when he hit on the happy idea of describing the essential elements of marriage as "bona": as "GOOD THINGS". Thank God for Pope John Paul II when, in *Familiaris Consortio*, he speaks of indissolubility in terms of something joyful that Christians should announce to the world. "It is necessary", he says, "to reconfirm the *good news* of the definitive nature of conjugal love."[2]

Fidelity and offspring are good things. Indissolubility is good news! The Bishop of Hippo and the Roman Pontiff are making affirmations that spur us to think: to pursue a line of thought that can lead to discovery or rediscovery. To my mind, it is vital for the future of marriage and the family that we rediscover the something hidden here that is elementary, that should be all too obvious, but has become all too obscured: the simple fact that each of the "bona matrimonialia" is exactly that: a "quid *bonum*", a *good* thing. Each is "a good" because each contributes powerfully not only to the good of society, but also to the "bonum coniugum", to the "good" of the spouses, to their development and maturing as persons who have grown in worth and character and generosity: who have learned to love. (And that, of course, is the ultimate good that each of us needs to acquire and develop here on earth: the ability to love.)

It is natural to want an exclusive, permanent bond

Only when people recover this way of thinking will they properly understand that since these "bona" are good things, they are *desirable*; and *it is natural to want them*. It is natural, because it corresponds to the nature of human love. Man finds something deeply good in the idea of a love: (i) of which he is the privileged and singular object; (ii) which will be his for as long as life lasts; (iii) and through which, by becoming a co-creator, he can perpetuate himself (and, as we shall see, more than himself). Precisely because of the goodness which he sees

43

in these "goods", what is natural to man is not to fear or exclude them, but to seek and welcome them.

It is natural then to want an exclusive, permanent and fruitful marital union. It is *unnatural* to exclude any of these three elements. We need to get our thinking back into proper perspective so that we are hit by—and can hit others with— the fact of the natural goodness of these "goods" of marriage.

The good of fidelity or exclusiveness is clear: "You are *unique* to me". It is the first truly personalized affirmation of conjugal love; and echoes the words God addresses to each one of us in Isaiah: "Meus es tu"—"You are mine."[3]

The good of indissolubility should also be clear: the good of a stable home or haven: of knowing that this "belonging-ness"—shared with another—is for keeps. People want that, are made for that, expect that it will require sacrifices and sense that the sacrifices are worth it. "It is natural for the human heart to accept demands, even difficult ones, in the name of love for an ideal, and above all in the name of love for a person."[4] It is a strange head and heart that rejects the permanence of the marriage relationship.

For my present purposes, however, I will not enlarge on these two aspects, but wish rather to limit attention to the *bonum prolis*: the "good" or value of offspring.

Depriving oneself of goodness

The contraceptive mentality—probed into so painfully by the healing intent of *Humanae Vitae*—is an ailment that could prove fatal to Western society. Debate or disagreement about the specific morality of family planning *techniques* is not the heart of the matter: in itself, in fact, it is just one aspect of the overall pathological picture. The real sickness here is that practically our whole Western civilization has come to look on family limitation as a good thing and fails to see that it is the *privation* of a good thing.

I am not thinking here of those couples who, for health reasons, economic factors, etc., really need the help of natural family planning (and have recourse to it with regret). I am thinking of those others—the very many others—who could afford to have a larger family, and freely choose not to, without apparently realizing the *goodness* of what they are thus *depriving* themselves of. They prefer to have less of the "bona matrimonialia", less in particular of the "good" of offspring, so as to have more of material goods. And the quality of their life—more and more materialized, less and less humanized—flows inevitably from their choice. Material goods cannot hold a marriage together; matrimonial goods, especially the "good" of offspring, can.

There is indeed something profoundly good in that specific aspect of conjugal sexual union in which is to be found its true uniqueness: the sharing together not so much in what may or may not be a unique pleasure, as in what *is* a unique *power*: a power—the result of sexual complementarity—to bring about a new life. Man and woman have a deep desire for such a true conjugal sexual union; and that desire is thoroughly rooted in human nature.

It seems particularly important today to underline, in all its fullness, the *personalist* thrust of this natural desire, which goes beyond any desire for either mere self-assertion or mere self-perpetuation.

Self-assertion? Self-perpetuation?

Contraceptive sexual intercourse between spouses can be merely self-assertive: each one seeking himself or herself, and failing truly to find or know or give to the other. True marital sexual intercourse, open to life, is—of its very nature—*love*-assertive. It asserts mutual conjugal love and donation, precisely in the uniqueness and greatness of the shared sexual potential of the spouses.

The desire for self-perpetuation is something natural which in itself already has a deep personalist value. (If modern man does not readily grasp or feel this, it is a sign of the extent to which he is humanly de-vitalized, de-naturalized and de-personalized.) Conjugality, however, takes the procreative sexual urge beyond the natural wish to perpetuate just *oneself*. In the context of conjugal love, this natural desire for self-perpetuation also acquires new scope and meaning. It is no longer a matter of two separate selves, each wishing—perhaps in a selfish way—for self-perpetuation. It is rather the case of

45

two persons in love, who naturally want to perpetuate *the love* that draws them to one another, so that they can have the joy of seeing it take flesh in a new life, fruit of that mutual spiritual and carnal knowledge by which they express their spousal love.[5]

Two persons in love want to do things together: to design or make or buy or furnish together something that will be peculiarly *theirs*, because it is the fruit of their united decision and action. Nothing, we repeat, is more proper to a couple than their child. The sculptor hews his vision of beauty into lasting stone. Only parents can create *living* works of art, with each child a unique monument to the creative love that inspires and unites them.

A society, through the monuments it builds, evokes the memory of the great things of its past, in order to keep its values alive in the present and for the future. Spousal love needs such monuments. When romance is fading, when perhaps it has died and the spouses are tempted to think that love between them has died with it, then each child remains as a living testimony to the depth and uniqueness and totality of the conjugal gift of self which they made to each other in the past—when it was easy—and as an urgent call to keep giving now, even when it is hard.

Planned absences

In my work at the Roman Rota, I not infrequently come across petitions of annulment of what clearly are perfectly genuine marriages of couples who married out of love, but whose marriages collapsed fundamentally because they deliberately delayed having children and thus deprived their married love of its natural support.

If two people remain just looking ecstatically *into* each other's eyes, the defects that little by little they are going to discover there can eventually begin to appear intolerable. If they gradually learn to look *out* together at their children, they will still discover each other's defects, but they will have less time or reason to think them intolerable. They cannot however look out together at what is not there.

A series of *planned absences* is turning the married life of many couples today into a hollowed-out reality, a vacuum that eventually collapses in on itself. A married couple can stare the love out of each other's eyes. If married love is to grow, it has to contemplate, and be contemplated by, other eyes—many pairs of eyes—born of that very love.[6]

Conjugal love, then, needs the support represented by children.[7] Children strengthen the *goodness* of the bond of marriage, so that it does not give way under the strains that follow on the inevitable wane or disappearance of effortless romantic love. The bond of marriage—which God wants no man to break—is then constituted not just by the variables of personal love and sentiment between husband and wife, but more and more by their children, each child being one further strand giving strength to that bond.

In his homily in Washington, DC, in October 1979, Pope John Paul II reminded parents that "it is certainly less serious to deny their children certain comforts or material advantages than to deprive them of the presence of brothers and sisters, who could help them to grow in humanity and to realize the beauty of life at all its ages and in all its variety."[8] I would suggest to parents who too easily incline to family limitation, to read the Pope's reminder in the light of the Vatican II teaching that "children are the *supreme* gift of marriage and contribute to the *greatest* extent to the good of the *parents* themselves."[9] It is therefore not only their present children, but also *themselves*, that such parents may be depriving of a singular "good", of a unique experience of human life, the fruit of love.

Educated choices

One frequently comes across statements to the effect that "family planning or limitation is more easily accepted by people as they get better educated." Whether we realize it or not, to admit such statements unquestioningly is to concede a whole philosophy of life. A very particular type of education thoroughly imbued with a very particular kind of values (or rather of anti-values), is necessary before people are brought to the point of easily accepting family limitation. Can such education be regarded as Christian education? Can it be

47

regarded as *true* education at all? It is worth recalling the judgment that Newman, some one hundred and forty years ago, passed on the education of his time. Modern man, he said, is instructed, but not educated. He is taught to do things, and to think enough so as to do them; but he is not taught to think more. . . .[10]

This whole issue is one of values and choices: of goods and options. Few people can have all the goods of this world. But most people have a certain choice. I can choose *good A* or *good B*, though possibly not both. Then I have to choose between them. The wise and properly human choice takes the *better* good, and *knows* it is richer in choosing so: that is the educated choice. The less human or less wise choice opts for the inferior good; and probably does not know it is duping and impoverishing itself. There is a forceful passage in the Bible which is not altogether without relevance here: "I have set before you life and death, blessing and curse; therefore choose life, that you and your descendants may live."[11] There is no half-way choice between life and death. What, one may ask, is the real term of the choices the Western world is making?

In Kenya a couple of years ago, an African who had learned that the Western fertility rate averages about 1.2, remarked to me: "Western couples must be *very poor* if they can't afford to have more than two children . . . ." He was not a qualified "expert" in the Western sense; yet his words may be worth pondering. They could be complemented with another bit of "non-expert" wisdom, this time from the West itself. I knew a recently married couple some time back in England, a normal couple who wanted children. One child was born; but then there was an unwanted delay of three or four years. At last the mother became expectant again. Their first-born too was filled with expectations. But—a miscarriage occurred. The father had to tell the child he was not going to have that little brother or sister he wanted. "Look; Mom's not going to have that baby after all"; and, bowing before God's inscrutable ways, he added, "it's better that way . . . ." The kid however didn't bow so easily: "But, Daddy, is there *anything better* than a baby? . . ."[12] Computerised programs never anticipate the things that children come up with. The wisdom of children is part of the "bonum prolis". . . .

The child in that episode had a true *sense of values*: which, according to *Humanae Vitae*, is precisely the first thing a married couple need to possess if they are to approach family planning correctly.[13] A true sense of values is not shown by the couple who fail to see that a child is the best acquisition they can make, and the one that enriches them most.

Many married couples in the West no longer seem to realize the simple truth that children are the most personalized fruit of their own conjugal love; and are therefore the greatest gift they can make to one another, being at the same time God's gift to both of them.

"But—if we have an extra child, our children and we ourselves will be less well-off . . . ." You will hardly say that the extra child will be less well off, unless you wish to rank yourself among those who wonder whether life itself is a good thing, or whether non-existence may not after all be preferable to existence.

"But our other children—those we have already—will be worse off . . . ." Will they? The Pope suggests that, in terms of truly human values, they will not.

"But, we ourselves . . . we will be less well-off. We will have a tougher time . . . ." You may have to work harder, that is true (many people work very hard today so as to have material "goods"), but will what you are working for make you less happy?

In seminars, when this matter comes up, I have at times asked my students to consider a small matter of comparative analysis. It goes something like this:

	Children	Cars	TV/VCR	Education of children	Holiday abroad
FAMILY A:	2	2	2/2	Good or best schools	Yes
FAMILY B:	5	1	1/0	Second-rate schools	Never

After putting this on the board, my first question to the students is: Which family has the higher standard of living? They all answer: Family A, of course. So I repeat the question: Which family has the higher standard of living? There may be the slightest hesitation, but they repeat the same answer. So I repeat the same question again, and a third, and perhaps a fourth time. Perplexity sets in, hesitations grow, until in the end someone "concedes": "well, of course, if you start considering children as *part* of your standard of life . . . ."

"If you start". . . . It is indeed time that we started putting children down on the assets side, and not on the liabilities. On *both*, you say? OK; on both: like your motor car. A car is an asset *and* a liability. It costs money and effort and attention to acquire and to maintain: just as a child does. Your choice should begin by considering which is worth more, because to choose the other is to lower one's own standard of living.[14]

"Which will give me more satisfaction?" is no doubt a utilitarian rather than an idealistic viewpoint. Yet, even if a person wishes to apply that view to our subject, he or she would do well to consider the money and time and effort that people nowadays put into golf or computers or creative gardening, *working* at them, *reading* all about them, in search of a satisfaction they do not always get.

How come they do not think parenthood worth working at? How is it they do not study books (there are plenty available) on how to enjoy caring for one's children, on the satisfactions of being a parent? And how is it (our horizons broaden again) they do not sense the call of an utterly unique creativity, the adventure of being co-creators?

Somewhere deep in their hearts, couples probably do sense the truth of the fact that a child is a good and a great gift. The trouble is that they have been conditioned not to *trust* that truth. They have to be helped to trust it; and clearly (at least to my mind), it is only couples who have chosen the "good" of offspring—in all the fullness with which God wished to bless their marriage—who can teach them. Pope Paul VI, in *Humanae Vitae*, took good care to mention such parents *first*, among those who live up to God's expectations for responsible parenthood and exercise it "by the deliberate and generous decision to raise a numerous family".[15]

So many marriages today are suffering from *self*-privation, a voluntarily induced impoverishment, brought about by a refusal of the gift of life and a rejection of the fruitfulness of love. Our modern well-off western society may go down in history as "the *deprived* society"; where people—entire peoples—ailed to death by having a sense of true human values gradually sucked out of their lives.

The loss of sexuality

A final word on this concept of privation. At times a privation may be wise and necessary, for instance when health reasons demand that a person abstain from solid food. But it is none the less a privation. And, if it is not to end in death, it must be a temporary measure, so that the patient can get back to being nourished by a normal and healthy appetite. The western appetite for sex today is not normal; nor is it healthy; nor, as I suggested in the last chapter, is it really sexual.

The proponents of contraception reject the Church teaching that the procreative and unitive aspects of conjugal sex are inseparable, and maintain that it is perfectly alright to separate them. But that is *not* what contraception actually does. Its real effect is not to separate these two aspects (with the implication that, though it annuls the procreative, it respects the unitive), but to *destroy both*. Contraceptive sex is not procreative: that is clear to everyone.What is not so clear to people is that it is not unitive, in any conjugal sense.The ultimate analysis, however, tells us that it is *not* sex, in any real human sense, at all.

What is being separated is not sex from some element extraneous to sex; or even from some element peculiarly connected by an unfortunate accident of biological design to sex. What is being separated is the action of sex—the *apparent* action of sex—from the *meaning* of sex. The reality of sex is being totally put aside; and people are being left with a mere pantomime of sex.

What is being separated is the very "body" of sex from the "soul" of sex; and what is being left is the corpse of sex.What contraception gives people is *apparent* "body-sex", that is actually soul-less sex. It is mummified sexuality: dead sex. Our modern world is busy in the process of killing human sex and sexuality.

Many modern marriages are lacking a true sexual appetite. The sexuality marking them is not a truly human sexuality. A maimed masculinity and a maimed femininity are meeting in no authentic conjugal encounter. Such marriages, denied the essential humanizing and personalizing qualities of true conjugal sex—denied the true "bonum sexualitatis": the true "good" of sexuality—are in danger of death by conjugal-sexual starvation. A self-imposed barrenness is denying their love the fruit which love itself is designed to produce, and which it needs for its own nourishment and survival.

4   *Divorce: husband and wife*

As pointed out in the Introduction, divorce is today regarded by most persons in Western countries as one of the marks of progressive societies. Hence no doubt the surprise, and even the scandal, of so many at the rejection of divorce by the Irish people just a few years ago.

Here let us insist on the point that one can logically regard divorce as progress only if one is convinced that it is a means to greater happiness. Does divorce bring about more happiness? Does it make for happier persons, for happier families and happier societies? If in fact it makes the majority of people happier, even though it may perhaps leave a minority less happy, then one can perhaps reasonably maintain that it represents progress. But if it is the other way round, if it makes a minority happier, but makes the majority less and less happy, then divorce represents the opposite of progress. I would suggest that this in fact is the actual situation, and moreover that one can check this for oneself by means of a little clear thinking plus a look at a few concrete facts.

That marriage is indissoluble of its nature was taught explicitly by Jesus Christ.[1] Our Lord's teaching has been re-echoed and solemnly confirmed time and again by the Catholic Church.[2] The Church therefore teaches that every true marriage (whether sacramental or not) is indissoluble. My purpose is not to restate this unvarying teaching, but rather to suggest: a) that divorce, even on the level of individual and earthly happiness, tends to do more harm than good; and, b) that indissolubility, far from being an enemy of human love or a restraint on human fulfillment is meant to be their support and bulwark. The arguments backing each of these affirmations complement one another, and at times are identical. The first can be dealt with briefly enough; the second merits greater attention.

Divorce does not tend to make for happiness. Divorce tends to make for divorce; and divorce always marks the final collapse of a hope of happiness. Divorce, it is frequently argued, is only meant for the hard cases—for those persons whose marriages have in fact failed—so as to give them the chance to start again. The evidence, however, is becoming massive that the remedy is worse than the illness.

Divorce is not curing hard cases; it is creating them. Divorce breeds divorce; and it breeds and multiplies fast. It is a simple matter of fact that once divorce is allowed in a society, its incidence spirals upwards. The following figures bring out how the matter has developed in the U.S.A. over two thirty-year periods from 1900 to 1960. They show the relationship between the number of marriages celebrated and the number of divorces granted in the same year: the relationship, so to speak, between the number of marriages "made" and those "unmade" in a given year.

Year	Marriage	Divorces	% of divorces to marriages
1900	709,000	56,000	8%
1930	1,127,000	196,000	17%
1960	1,527,000	395,000	26%[3]

The upward spiral continued and accelerated dramatically. The 1960 proportion had all but doubled only fifteen years later. In 1975, the number of marriages was 2,126,000, and of divorces, 1,026,000[4]: practically a 50% proportion. One divorce for every two marriages celebrated!

This can scarcely be described as a picture of increasing human happiness. It rather gives clear evidence of growing human failure and isolation. Of all natural institutions, marriage—with its hope of a love that is stable, deep and permanent—surely offers the greatest promise of happiness. If, in divorcist societies, up to 50% of persons who marry fail to find happiness in marriage, where are they going to find it? In a second marriage? The statistics again say No. The divorce rate, among divorcees who re-marry, is three or four times higher than among those who marry for the first time.

It is easy enough to see how the legalization of divorce tends to create a situation that drives more and more marriages on the rocks. In a society where marriage is regarded as an irrevocable step, people think twice or three times about marrying. No one enters lightly on a life-long commitment. And later on in married life, when the inevitable difficulties come, the very fact that there is no "easy way out", helps them to fight to make a go of it. In a divorcist society, it is hard for people who marry not to have the thought somewhere in the back of their minds, "If it doesn't work, I can always get a divorce." With such an approach, there is nothing definitive about the step of getting married. One is not committing one's life, one is simply trying something out, while reserving to oneself the "right" to get out of it or to get rid of it, if it does not work. The divorcist mentality breeds a *commercial* approach to marriage. One tends, from the outset to regard the whole transaction with certain misgivings, and therefore one insists on a "freedom-back-if-not-satisfied" guarantee. "Try it, just to see" may be a sound basis to a business transaction. Is it a sound basis to what should be a transaction of love? An "I'll try it, to see" approach to marriage is an essentially calculating attitude, and is almost certain to bring about failure; because one may try it, but one does not try *oneself*.

Indissolubility and happiness

My second suggestion was that indissolubility is designed (by Nature, by God) to make for human happiness, not to spoil it. Now, we can understand the point of indissolubility, if we understand the point of marriage itself. Marriage is designed to make people happy, by *teaching them to love*; indissolubility is simply God's rule for those *apprenticed to love*: that they are not entitled to give up the effort to love even when it becomes difficult. Let us take a deeper look into this.

Marriage (and indissolubility), we have just stated, should make people happy because this is part of God's design for marriage. A few evident qualifications need to be added to this statement:

—although marriage can and should make people happy, it cannot make them perfectly happy. Perfect happiness cannot be found here on earth. It can only be found in Heaven. So, if one insists on expecting perfect happiness from marriage, one is *bound* to be disappointed;[5]

—secondly and equally important, although marriage can make people happy, it cannot make them *effortlessly* happy. Happiness is not found easily; it takes an effort. Easy happiness does not last. This means there is no such thing as a happy marriage without an effort;[6]

—from the general principle, "marriage should make people happy", one should not too quickly or too easily draw the particular conclusion, "marriage should make *me* happy". If made in strict logic, the conclusion follows. But if made — as it so often is — in a spirit of impatience, self-pity, bitterness or indignation, it is almost certainly proceeds less from logic than from self-centeredness. And marriage, if approached self-centeredly, is just not going to work, i.e. is not going to make anyone happy.

Each one of these points, especially the last, merits some further comment.

Marriage cannot give perfect happiness. That is not its purpose. Its purpose, one could say, is not to give the spouses perfect happiness, but to *mature* them for perfect happiness. In everything here on earth, God is trying to teach us to love — so that we will be able to enjoy Heaven fully. Marriage is one of his most intensive schools of love, and the one where He tries to train most of his pupils.

This is where the second point comes in. If marriage takes an effort, it is because love takes an effort. Love is no easy subject to learn; just the contrary. The reason for its difficulty lies in the fact that we are all strongly self-centered. Love, true love, is other-centered. As a result, the average self-centered person (i.e. all of us) has to overcome his or her selfishness in order to be able to love. And this means a constant effort and struggle: a struggle that can go up and down, see-saw like. Love will grow only if self-centeredness is lessened. If selfishness remains, love cannot grow. If selfishness grows, love declines and can die. Love seldom dies a natural death. If it dies, it is normally because it has been murdered: killed by self-love.

We are strongly self-centered, but not totally so. We have in fact a real hankering and need for true love, for other-centeredness. But it is true that in practically all marriages, each of the spouses starts out with a much larger dose of self-centeredness than of other-centeredness.

But—it may be objected—surely two people who marry are usually very much in love, and therefore very "other-centered"? Perhaps they are, perhaps they are not; time alone will tell. How is it that so many persons who, on marrying, regarded their partner as the "only one in the world", eight or ten years later "can't stand" him or her, and get divorced? Their love "died", we are told; and divorce is the only logical step once love has died. We will consider in a moment what may be the best thing to do, if love had "died". But let us not proceed too soon. We could profitably do a post-mortem on this married love that—we are told—has just died, remembering again that if love dies, it seldom dies a sudden death.

Love, at the time of the marriage, was aglow with health. Through what peculiar process of consumption and decline has it passed that one or both of the spouses want to write its obituary notice ten or fifteen years later? Was it, after all, not as strong and healthy as appeared at the start? Probably not. Love seldom *starts* strong, for at the start one seldom knows the other person well and in depth, i.e. as he or she really is (a mixture, like all of us, of good points and bad points).

What starts strong is romance. But romance tends to idealize the other person. It therefore is not really other-centered, for it is centered not on the *real* other, but on an "other" seen through rose-tinted glasses that reflect an image peculiarly pleasing to the viewer. Romance, in other words, is perfectly compatible with a large dose of self-centeredness.

Romance is pleasant and easy. It can give love an initial push to get it going, but it is not the same as love. And when the easy momentum that romance produces runs out, love—if it is there—has to keep going on its own. It is easy to "fall in love". To be in love, to remain in love, to stand in love, without falling "out" of it: all of this is difficult.

Romantic love sees no defects in the other person. Real love should see them, or at least be convinced that they are there and will appear. And real love must obviously love the other person with his or her defects: love him or her, that is, as he or she really is. That is anything but easy.[7]

A profession of love that is equivalent to "I love you provided you have no defects", is not love at all. It is the same as saying, "I'll love you provided you don't turn out to be a real person. . ."; and clearly, the love that is only prepared to love a fictional person is a fictional love. To put it another way: "I'll love you provided you have no defects" is the same as saying, "I'll love you provided I don't have to make an effort to love you. . ."—which is the approach of simple and sheer selfishness, no more.

Attaching conditions to love

That is why any conditions attached to love (especially the condition implied in allowing for the possibility of divorce) are a sign that self-centeredness is present, and well settled into a good defensive position. "I'll love you until December 31, 1997—and always provided I don't meet someone who attracts me more before then": that sounds like a good, straightforward, cards-on-the-table, commercial approach. It does not sound like love.

If marriage is viewed as a satisfaction-producing machine, the moment it no longer gives satisfaction, it has essentially failed and should be replaced; just as one replaces any other machine, such as a television set or a car, that no longer works satisfactorily. But is it the marriage that has failed, or is it the husband or the wife, or both of them? . . . When the car breaks down irremediably, was it destined to be a dud from the start, or was it simply the victim of bad driving? And how long will a new car last in the hands of the same driver unless he or she learns to drive properly?

You have to *learn* to love. You have to work at it. It takes time. And it can get harder as one goes on. But if one perseveres, one learns. This after all is the way we approach other major aspects of life: e.g. a business or a profession. The vast majority of people are quite convinced that to be successful as a doctor or lawyer or accountant, one has to study at some school or university for years; and, after graduation, still keep studying. And that even then, with years and years of con-

58

stant learning and effort, one may still not achieve all the professional success one had expected. The peculiar thing is that the same people appear to expect instant and effortless success or happiness in marriage; and when the need for effort emerges, they (if they have absorbed the divorcist mentality) seem to think that the reasonable thing is to quit. It is not. It would be just as reasonable to quit studying medicine at a particular university because one found the effort to master physiology or pharmacology too exacting, and to look around for another university where one could become a doctor without having to tire oneself studying these subjects. Even if such a person, by some fluke, graduated from some strange medical school, could he or she be anything but a failure as a doctor? Similarly, the person not prepared to make the effort to love—to *learn* to love—can only end up a failure as a husband or wife.

Happiness demands an effort. Marriage demands an effort. When a person in difficulties allows the thought, "I'll get a divorce and marry this other man/woman, because I'll be happier with him/her", what they are really saying, without realizing it, is: "My happiness depends on not having too much demanded of me. I'll be happy only if I don't have to give too much, only if I don't have to come out of myself, only if I don't have to make much of an effort to love. . . ." The person who lets himself think this way can never be happy. The reason is clear. Happiness is a consequence of giving: "it is happier to give than to receive." [8] Happiness is not possible—inside or outside marriage—for the person who is determined to get more than he is prepared to give.

Indissolubility then is really God's law for would-be quitters[9]: for those who get tired of the demands of love and fidelity, and are tempted to chicken out. God says No; He says, "Keep at it." The happiness game, which is no cakewalk, is demandingly but all-wisely refereed by God. When played within marriage, one of its main rules is indissolubility: you just don't quit the game when the play gets tough; if you quit, you lose.

I repeat: there is *no* easy way to happiness. Those who seek divorce because of the difficulties that marriage involves, are simply balking at the difficulties that happiness involves.

They are settling themselves on the road that leads away from happiness.

The biggest enemy of love is not the other person's selfishness, but one's own selfishness. One can run away from the other person, but one's own selfishness runs with one . . . . After all, it is possible to love a selfish person (God does). But it may be impossible for a selfish person to love.

The intervening decades scarcely call for a modification of the judgments of a 1967 *Newsweek* article on "The Divorced Woman". It pointed out how the divorcee is, self-confessedly, more selfish and more independent, though at the same time more self-conscious and socially more maladjusted: more defensive, *less expectant of happiness*, sadder. . . . "Her 'tristesse' is revealed in the incidence of divorced women seeking psychoanalysis, in their rate of alcoholism (one in four), and suicide (three times that of married women)."[10]

Bringing love back

The conjugal instinct which draws people to marry and makes them work for a happy marriage, also tends to make them work to heal a wounded marriage or to remake a broken one.

"I no longer love my husband (or my wife). My love for him (or her) has gone. . . ." Your love for him, which has gone, can come back. But, for this, you have to learn to forgive. If you had forgiven earlier (and perhaps also if you had asked for forgiveness), your love would not have died. It is not quarrels between husband and wife that destroy married love; it is the failure to make them up: the inability to forgive and to ask for forgiveness. Quarrels (even big ones) made up, do not destroy love; they can even cement it. Quarrels (even small ones) not made up, gradually poison married life and make it seem intolerable.

The love you once had has died. How much was it worth to you in the past? By what sacrifices did you show your sense of its worth? What did you do then to protect it? And, perhaps more importantly, how much are you prepared to give now in order to bring it back to life? Love can be kept alive, but not without sacrifice. Love can be brought back to life, but not without sacrifice.

"But—I'm not interested in reviving that love. My marriage was a failure, and I just don't care any longer for him or her." That very probably is not true. Married love is a great treasure: too great a treasure to be lost without regret. Go back to that conjugal instinct that led you to marry, and try to revive it in its purity and idealism and generosity.

The instinct to marry, after all, is not a selfish one, and few people marry out of purely selfish motives. Marriage has to be built on the generosity involved in that instinct: the generous urge to be a good husband or wife, to learn to love one's spouse, as he or she is, with his or her defects, the generous urge to swallow pride, to overlook hurtful things, to forgive and to forget. It is simply not christian, nor is it human either, to think that life is governed by an instinct always to get one's own back, to "to give tit for tat", to answer badness badly.

There is a special memory indelibly impressed on my mind from my one visit to the Grand Canyon. It has nothing to do with the awesome grandeur of Nature working on Nature over thirty million years. It has to do with a very tiny bit of humanity bawling his head off in the ecologically silent bus which brought us along the southern rim of the Canyon. The mother was fruitlessly using her patience to try to pacify the child. Whatever the reason for his three-year-old rage, it erupted into a brutal climax directed precisely against her. His shrill voice spitefully articulated each word: "I—*hate*—you. . . ." The shock and the hurt ripped through the bus, but the evil spell was broken by the mother's reply, which came quick and clear and true: "And—*I*—LOVE—you!"

But, it will be said: it is part of human nature, it is maternal instinct to love so. Quite. But it is human nature too, it is conjugal instinct, to want to be faithful in marriage, happen what may; to react with love for husband or wife, even when he or she does something hurtful or hateful.

It is the person who answers contempt or hate with love, that *wins*. Love is the secret weapon, it is always the stronger instrument; it has God's strength.

If you want to revive married love, go back and look again for the good points you thought your partner once had, and for which you once loved him or her. It is not likely that they have completely disappeared; but you need to concentrate on *re*-finding them. And, for that, you need to make the effort to keep his or her bad points out of your mind.

It can also help very much if you look for the good points which your partner's friends think he or she still has. In stress, don't seek opinion or advice about your partner from *your* friends: seek it from *his* friends, or from *hers*. Your friends will possibly not be able to help you to see your partner in a better and truer light; his or her friends—if you listen to them—very probably can do so.

Meaningless unions?

A final word about the "hopeless" cases. What to do, for instance, if one's partner really seems to have *no* virtues left? What if the husband is an absolute alcoholic, or the wife is completely mental? Even in such circumstances I have known cases, many cases, of persons who have kept faith, who have remembered the vows that love once inspired in them: "for better or for worse, in sickness or in health", and seeing their partner reduced to such a sad state of sickness and poverty, have responded to the challenge, and risen to a heroic height in loving.

The charge that the Church, if it refuses a divorce in such cases, is passing a sentence of unhappiness on a husband or wife, is simply not true, Such persons will not be unhappy, though they will undoubtedly suffer, if they try to bear such a cross in close union with Christ.

Naturally a further point must be made here. If a person feels that what is asked in such a situation is too much; if a wife, for instance, feels she can no longer live with a drunkard of a husband who physically mistreats her, then, in the last resort, separation can of course be granted.

So the Church is not denying the right to divorce, in *that* sense. But it is saying: you can separate from your husband or your wife, but you are still bound to him or her. Perhaps it would be better to express it this way. It is Our Lord who is in effect saying to that person: "You can separate from your husband or your wife. But do not separate from Me. You may feel you can no longer be happy with your partner. But you can be happy with Me. Be faithful to what I ask of you. Try to administer well the talent of fidelity I have entrusted to you. And your reward will be great."

There is no condemnation to unhappiness here. What there is, is a special call to holiness. Some people, it is true, rise to such a call well; others do not. Just as some people, stricken with cancer, rise to a new degree of love of God in accepting their illness, while others lapse into bitterness and resentment. This is simply part of the deep mystery of human freedom, and of our capacity to answer God's grace in different ways.

The idea that once a marriage has become burdensome, it has become "meaningless" and should be done away with through divorce, shares much of the same despairing outlook on life as the attitude which readily declares the sufferings of an incurable patient to be purposeless, and would put an end to them through euthanasia. All marriages, like all sickness, must come to an end some time. In that sense, they are all "terminal". But none need be meaningless. All of our earthly experiences, good and bad, come to an end. Or rather, it is our crosses which come to an end; an end which, if we have tried to bear those crosses well, is the beginning of our real happiness and eternal reward.

5 *Divorce: the children*

The last chapter sought to show how the marriage bond is designed to protect love, to keep the spouses' love in one piece, despite the wear and tear of daily life and the centrifugal forces of selfishness. But the unbreakable character of the marriage bond is designed not just to protect the love of the spouses alone, but also and very specially to protect love *for the children*: to prevent the atmosphere of love which they need for their development and happiness from being shattered by the weakness of one or both parents, by their selfishness or by their simple lack of thought.

That children have a right to their parents' fidelity has often been said; and that children are made unhappy by divorce is surely more than obvious. I would like to suggest a further perspective from which the matter of divorce can be considered.

In a divorce situation one can no doubt set up a plea for the children's right to happiness, as *against* the right to happiness which the parents claim or (more probably) which one of the parents claims for himself or herself. To me it seems more positive to go directly to that parent's heart and to try to help him or her to weigh his or her own happiness and his or her children's happiness *together*, so as to see that they cannot be separated: that the happiness of the children (the easier happiness that the children are entitled to) and their parents' happiness (the tougher happiness that the parents should be prepared to live) are so interlinked that one cannot stand without the other.

A married person has fallen "out of" love with his or her spouse, and "into" love with a third party. He or she thinks of divorce and would justify the possibility in the name of *"my right to happiness"*. That such a person is thinking selfishly is less to our point than the fact that he or she is not thinking clearly. That person's right to happiness will not be satisfied by a divorce, because a divorce harms too many things that are essential to his or her happiness. It shatters his or her children's happiness; and that effectively undermines the divorced parent's happiness too.

A heart divided about happiness

The situation needs adequate analysis. It is not enough to see a sort of external opposition of "happinesses", as if the person were caught in a cross-fire between his or her personal right to happiness and his or her children's right to happiness. Nor is it enough to say that husband and wife should be prepared to sacrifice their personal happiness to that of their children. There is truth in that; but it is only part of the truth. Such an analysis does not go deep enough.

The real point is that his or her own heart is divided in itself precisely about personal happiness. That heart is torn between two conflicting considerations about happiness; and unless the tension is resolved properly, he or she will never be happy.

On the other hand there is the thought, "I won't be happy if I have to continue living with my husband or wife" (and—perhaps—"I won't be happy unless I can live with X, whom I now feel I love") . . . . On the other hand, there is the thought, "But I won't be happy without my children's love either! . . ."

This last point has to be considered in its full implications. Because a person may argue: "But, I can divorce and still have my children with me—at least most or part of the time"; or, "I can divorce, and still love my children. I can divorce and still have my children's love."

This is where reasoning loses touch with reality. A divorced person may retain partial or total custody of their children. What they will not retain is the children's love, certainly not all of it. At the best, they will retain a very reduced part of it, for the very fact of divorce inevitably destroys a large part of that love. That is why it is fooling oneself to think, "Even if I get a divorce, I'll still love my children, as before; and they'll still love me, as before." It is just not true; if you divorce, things can never be as before. They won't love you as before; they will love you, at best, with a maimed love, with the same sort of love that you showed them in divorcing. If your love for them is not prepared for sacrifice, their love for you will be without respect.

65

When a marriage has remained childless, husband or wife has little defence against the temptation to see divorce as the easy way out of difficulties and the easy way into happiness. But once a married person has become a *parent*, there is no easy way out of difficulties and no easy way into happiness. Unless their children mean absolutely nothing to them, such parents have only one way to happiness: a way that goes *through* those difficulties.

Only where there is *no* love for the children is divorce the easy way out. But then it is the way out for a loveless person who, when they take that way, will carry their lack of love with them.

Where there are children and where there is love for them, the temptation of divorce puts every quality and resource a person has to the test. Some people come out victorious from the struggle, some come out defeated. Many defeats, with their train of sadness, could be avoided if people were helped to think more clearly about the issues and the forces involved.

The issue is happiness—for *all concerned*. And the forces—the forces at work right there within the heart of the person tempted to divorce—are basically two. One force—a powerful and, perhaps, seemingly irresistible force—thrusting against the marriage; a voice repeating insistently, "I cannot stand my partner. I cannot keep it up any longer." At the same time and in the same heart, however, there is force thrusting in favor of the marriage, in favor of the home of which *I* am father or mother, in favor of *my* children. There is another voice repeating with equal insistence, "I cannot let my children down. I cannot destroy their love."

Two forces fighting each other. Two voices struggling to be heard, each trying to shout the other down. One is the voice of tiredness: "I've had enough." It is the voice of self-concern and self-pity: of surrender. The other is the voice of generosity and loyalty: "You've got someone besides yourself to think of. Keep fighting." Two forces fighting inside. Which will win?

The voice of tiredness has its arguments. "But—it is better for the children if we separate. That way they won't be exposed to these continuous quarrels between us which do them such harm." The fault with this argument is that it does not present all the alternatives. It is bad for children to be

66

exposed to their parents' quarrels. It is better for them not to be so exposed. But it is *worse* for them to be exposed to their parents's divorce. One has reflected little on life if one has not realized that it is more damaging for a child to lose a parent through divorce than to lose him or her through death.

All the love my children need

If a person thinking of divorce is capable of thinking clearly, he or she will realize: divorce may be easier on *me*, but it can never be better for my children. What is good for children, what is best for them, is that their parents—the father and mother of the family they belong to; and no substitute father or mother—live together, in deliberate and faithful union, if not in perfect harmony.

"But that is impossible. In our case, it is impossible. The way he or she goes on. It drives me mad. . . . No, no. We cannot live together, not even with a minimum of external harmony."

You can't live together? It depends on how strong your motives are. If you are really concerned about your children and about what is best for them, then—with prayer, with God's help—you may yet learn to live together, at least with that minimum of external harmony. You cannot live together? You can try—for your children's sake.

"No, No. I can't do it." (And then comes a further "argument"): "And in any case I do love my children. Even if divorced, I'll give them all the love I gave them before. I'll give them all the love they need . . . . "

Don't you realize that the love they need is not just father's love in isolation, or mother's love in isolation? It is not just your love alone that they need; it is his love or her love as well. The love they need is their parents's love: *both* your loves *together*, your united love: father's and mother's love irrevocably put together and held sacred against every effort to pull them apart.

"What God has joined together, let no man put asunder."[1] The divine prohibition applies to divorce in more ways than one. It is also, and very particularly, that united parental love for their children which man—the parents themselves—must not tear apart. You cannot be united in your love for one another? You can be united in your love for your children.

The children need his or her love, as well as mine. This is what God wants you to reflect. This is what your own very heart wants you to face up to: *our* children need *our* love, they are entitled to it. If you still doubt that this is true, ask *them*: whether they prefer two loves apart, or two loves together: their parents' love.

Nevertheless, some parents contemplating divorce not only do not realize the truth of this, they even think that what the children need can easily be supplied in a substitute form. "My children need a father's or a mother's love, as well as my love? Well, of course, they can have it. Jim or Mary —whom I mean to marry once I am free—will make such a wonderful new parent; a much better parent, in fact, than that insensitive and intolerable Joe or Jane whom I've been putting up with all these years."[2]

They do not realize that for their children this can never be so. Jim or Mary may be liked by the children; or they may not. They may become good friends to them; or they may not. What they can never be or become is a father or mother.

The fact is that Joe or Jane, however insensitive or intolerable, *is* their father or mother: the one they have and the one they need: defects and all.

"But"—I hear the reply—"you don't know Joe. His drunken bouts. The way he treats the children when he is in that state. How can that be good for the children?" It's not. But your divorce will be worse. *Your* faithfulness will do them far more good than his drunkenness can do them harm. And your unfaithfulness will do them far more harm.

The lessons parents teach their children

Parents are meant not just to hug and kiss their children or buy them presents or merely feed them and pay their school fees. They are meant to teach them, to prepare them for life. And you can teach them marvelously by sticking with that intolerable husband or wife. You can teach them also through your failures. Because of course you will have some failures. Even with those failures—provided you start again each time—

you are still helping your children, and helping them immensely. You, in those precise and difficult circumstances, are doing a wonderful job as a father or mother. You are teaching them two most important lessons for life:

—that certain things are sacred in life, and marriage is one of them; that marriage is for keeps, until death;
—that marriage, which is meant to be a lasting union, is a union of two ordinary persons, with plenty of defects. Marriages don't last because two people are perfectly matched, because they are ideally suited to one another in temperament, because they have never had a row, never experienced difficulty in getting on. . . . No; marriages last because people set their minds to it, because they learn to get on.

How important it is for a young person entering adult life, and especially when approaching marriage, to be able to say: "My parents' marriage lasted. They stuck together. And it is not as if they always found it easy; not as if they were ideally matched. No way! They had their defects (we children too knew them: mom's nerves, dad's binges . . .). And yet they stuck together—perhaps mainly for our sake. I think they stuck together too because they prayed. They had their quarrels, but they were faithful."

How this steadies and strengthens young people who are themselves approaching marriage. They will not want to be less good than their parents; and they will know that this is not easy. And so they will think twice or three times about the marriage they are now beginning to contemplate. This boy, this girl. . . . Will it last between us? And when the voice comes inside—"Does it matter so much? If it does not work, you can always take the easy way out"—they will be more likely to reply, as a human heart should: "But I don't want the easy way out. My parents didn't want it; or at least they didn't take it. I want a marriage that works. I want a love that lasts. I can see plenty of people around me, and not too much older than myself, who have taken the easy way out. And what an unhappy and unholy mess they seem to be making of their lives. I don't want that."

This is the big lesson about marriage that is taught to children by the fidelity—under strain—of their parents. What is it, however, that is taught to their children, what sort of image of marriage is communicated to them, by parents who give way to the divorce temptation? Marriage—they are in effect telling their children—is a consumer commodity, not only liable to breakdown, but simply not worth repairing if it does break down. It is not really repairable at all. You just dump it as soon as it begins to go wrong, and go off and get a new one.

A husband or a wife? Well, that is something you acquire, as you might a motor-car. You choose an attractive model, one that you find comfortable, easy to use, demanding a minimum of effort on your part; but that you abandon once it gets old or a bit rattly, and starts being more trouble than it is worth. Basically it is worth very little. So you just look around for a "better" model and trade the old one in.

And, what if there are children in the marriage? Well, hopefully they'll enjoy the whole new transaction (after all, why can't they see it can be fun to change parents?). And if they don't, they'll have to grin and bear it. I'm their parent? Sure; but, to be honest, they were never really very important in my eyes. Just accessories that came with that original purchase I made. So, well, after all, that's it, that is what they are: just accessories. . . . The main thing is that *I* must be happy with *my* automobile. And if the old accessories don't fit or won't go with the new model, well then, regretfully and all, you know, I'll have to let them go. They don't mean all *that* to me.

That is the idea of marriage that divorced parents teach their children. And when those children marry, and the moment comes (it will come; it always comes) when *their* marriage becomes difficult, how will those children react? What sort of persons will they turn out to be in that moment? In all predictable certainty, they will be like their parents: "Why should I try to make a go of my marriage now that the going has become tough? Why should I sacrifice myself for my children? Children don't care for their parents" (oh yes, you cared—once—very much for your parents; and then they let you down and made you bitter). "Children don't respect their parents; at least I never respected mine" (but you did— right up to their divorce). . . .

Divorce casts a spell of unhappiness on children. And as the experience of that unhappiness mounts, there comes a growing bitterness towards their unfaithful parents.

So, in this divorce you are considering, it is not just your children's present happiness that is at stake; it is their future happiness too: the sort of life that you prepared them for, the sort of happiness—easy or difficult, true or false—that you, by your own life and example, taught them to seek. It is not just your marriage that is at stake; it is also their marriage in the future. Dump your marriage (and your family) now; and you are sinking your children's marriage tomorrow.

People contemplating divorce need to reflect on these realities—of which they may be only hazily aware. The choice they are faced with is not one between "freedom with happiness" on the one hand, and "condemned to misery", on the other.

What they are faced with is a choice between two approaches to happiness. The first is difficult: to remain stuck (i.e. faithful) to their present marriage and family. The second seems easy: to be "freed".

What they may or may not see is that the second choice is not a choice for happiness at all. It frees them from too many things. It "frees" them from the duty of loving someone they once promised to love, but who no longer seems lovable; but it also "frees" them from the right and privilege of being loved by those whose love they surely still want but no longer merit: their own children.

That is why the second choice is not a choice for happiness; or, if one wishes, it is a choice for such a poor "happiness" that it can never really make a person happy. It is a "profit-and-loss" happiness: calculated indeed, but badly calculated, because what has to be assigned to the loss column is just too great. It will be a happiness headed for quick bankruptcy because it has been acquired at too high a personal cost.

This chapter and the preceding one have been written for couples who sense that their marriage is breaking up. The last chapter was designed to help them reflect on *conjugal* fidelity: on the many motives for renewing or reviving the love that once brought their marriage into existence. But pastoral experience has of course taught me that with many couples it may seem too late to invoke that argument. It may be little use to appeal to a love that once existed but that is now (so they feel) dead beyond recovery. Even in such cases, nevertheless, one can and should appeal to the love that *is still there*: to their love for their children. That has been the purpose of this chapter: to appeal to *parental* fidelity. The motive of the children is *the* big motive for faithfulness: to keep a marriage together, whatever the effort.[3]

If the spouses make up their minds not to desert their children, God will not desert them. If they are prepared to make the effort to get on together, or at least to tolerate one another, then all the basis is laid for a possible—though gradual—*resurrection* of their love for one another.

So often estranged parents, who determine to work together *for their children*, to bury their differences and keep them buried, little by little rediscover respect for one another, because each is aware that the other is making a sacrifice; and from respect can come a new birth of love. The love they thought dead and gone for ever, revives.

I am sacrificing myself for my children. So is he or she. *We* are doing what we can for our children. And so the sense of joint purpose, of reunited endeavour, emerges. And gradually, if they persevere, this leads to renewed respect. Respect gives rise to renewed esteem. And esteem to reborn love.

In all of this I have not mentioned what is surely the toughest case of all: where one of the parents has made a definitive break, and has already divorced and remarried someone else. What is the abandoned party to do? *Not* to abandon the children; and a clear way of abandoning them is for him or her also to think of remarriage. If one parent has torpedoed the family, let the other not finally sink it. The remaining parent will certainly have to find a lot of extra strength somewhere. God alone can give it; but He will readily do so. If that parent prays, he or she will find the grace to give to the children the example of faithfulness— faithfulness, precisely, to an unfaithful husband or wife—that can still help the children to keep the ideal of marriage (which also means the demanding reality of marriage) before them.

Parents, children and the rules of life

Washington, DC, 1956. The comment came from a girl recently converted to Catholicism. In a mixture of relief and joy she said to me,"The thing is, Father, you just have no idea how tough it is when you don't know the rules of life. Now at last, I know them . . . ."

Her comment often comes back to me when I look at so many people today, especially so many young people, who really just don't seem to know the rules of life. I suppose that, deep down inside, they must find the going very tough (however much they may try to hide it).

Their lives certainly don't seem to offer much hope of working out well. How could they ?—lives lacking in faith, in ideals, in purity, in love; lives lacking, above all, in criterion, in the ability to distinguish between good and evil, between right and wrong.

Many parents—all of those at least who really love their children—are frightened at this panorama. Their fear is understandable. And it is understandable too that when they think of their own children (who are still perhaps very young), they ask themselves: How can we avoid this happening to our children?

How can it be avoided? By forming them! By forming their conscience; so that they have standards, so that they know the rules, so that they can distinguish between right and wrong. And by forming their will, so that they can fight.

CONSCIENCE IN CHILDREN

A four- or five-year-old child is already able to realize that some things are right or wrong. He easily realizes, for instance, that it is wrong to do something displeasing to persons whom he knows are good. If his parents are good, he knows he does wrong if he does something they do not like. Here we see how the groundwork is already being laid for his moral life.

The next step is very important and, if the parents are good, is easily taken. It is so important for it relates this incipient moral conscience to the supernatural world. It helps the child see that life implies a personal relationship towards an ever-present God—who wants to be our Friend—and that moral living means keeping friendship with that God.

We are speaking of the case of children whose parents are good (i.e. who want to be good and who are *fighting* to be good, which is the only practical way we have of "being good" in this life). If such parents teach their child that *God is good*—and if he can see, from his parents' way of acting, that they really believe this—then he will immediately know he does wrong if he does something that the good God does not want. He will realize too that he must struggle—as his parents are struggling—to behave well, to please the good God, *precisely because he is good.*

One could not over-stress how important it is that the child grasps this initial idea of what constitutes good and evil, right and wrong. He should be taught that something is *right* because it pleases a good God, and that something is wrong because it displeases this good God. That this is the only foundation for a sound and healthily formed moral conscience surely becomes obvious if one thinks of that other foundation that is far too often laid: "You have got to do what your parents tell you, because if you don't they will punish you" or: "We have got to do what God commands us because if we don't he will punish us."

Love at the foundation—or fear?

There is a complete contrast between these two foundations. And there is a complete contrast, too, between the alternative types of conscience and moral outlook built up on them. One alternative is a moral life based on love, that is, a truly Christian moral life such as is proposed to us on every page of the Gospel. The other alternative is a moral life based on fear. This latter type of life can never be truly Christian for it is lacking in that essential trust peculiar to the person who realizes he is a child of God.

74

If one feels tempted to reflect that it is this latter moral attitude, with all its defects, that seems most prevalent in many souls, then it is wise to remember how it can so easily originate. Parents therefore should see what a tremendously delicate and responsible mission they have in forming their children's conscience. The outcome, after all, depends so much on how good they are or are trying to be, on the trust in God our Father that they live and communicate to their children, on the atmosphere of love, and not of repression or punishment, that predominates in their home.

By this last point I do not mean that children need not or ought not ever be punished. There are moments when punishment is necessary. But then it should be the consequence of deliberate reflection; never of an outburst of temper. It should be proportionate to the fault committed. And if possible (a bit of thought almost always makes it possible), it should be a formative rather than a punitive punishment. In other words, it should be imposed not mainly to hurt the "delinquent" but to help him understand why what he did was in fact wrong.

Children and sin

When and how should children be formed in an awareness of sin? We have already given a partial answer to this. Before going deeper into the matter, a few further preliminary comments may be useful. One cannot help remarking on the peculiarity of the fact that today, though we hear more and more about conscience, we seem to hear less and less about sin. A greater sensitivity to the voice of conscience should logically, one feels, lead to a greater sensitivity to sin: i.e. to the occasions when we disobey that voice. If it is not so in practice, surely this is a sign of the superficiality with which the whole subject of conscience tends to be treated nowadays?

There is an undeniable tendency today to speak less of personal sin. It so happens, moreover, that this tendency seems to grow acute when the subject of "children and sin" comes up for discussion. "Take care!", one seems to hear a chorus of voices. "Take care not to speak to children about sin. Talk about sin so easily does such harm to their normal psychological development!"

What can in fact of harm to a child's normal psychological development is ignorance in this matter. Once children are old enough to understand that a particular action can offend God, they should not be left in ignorance of the fact that such actions are sinful, for there is a real danger that they will develop a habit in that area; and the more time is let pass, the harder it will be to correct that harmful habit.

At times one gets the impression that the reason why some people are so reluctant to treat of the subject of sin with children is that they themselves were victims of that type of education which treats of sin in terms of punishment and of the relation of the soul with God in terms of fear. If this is so, it would certainly seem preferable that *they* should not treat of the subject with children (let others do it) because in all probability they will deform them, creating in them a conscience whose dominant principle is fear. And a conscience deformed in this way certainly does harm.

But what we saw earlier ought to make it clear that this is not how children should be taught to understand sin. They should be taught to understand it in the first place not as something worthy of punishment (which is a purely self-concerned view), but as something showing a lack of love (for it is an offense against Someone who is Good); that it shows ingratitude towards Someone who loves us infinitely; that this is why we should be sorry for it; and that it is so easily made up for because God's Love is always quick to pardon. Teaching about sin, if done in this way, is always formative. Therefore the sooner it is begun, the better.

Sin and things that are "wrong"

Is everything that is wrong a sin? Not necessarily. There are some (few) things that can be wrong without their "wrongness" involving moral evil, and therefore without their constituting a sin. Much of what people classify as bad manners falls into this category. Faults of this type may be *socially* wrong, but generally speaking they are not *morally* wrong. (They could of course constitute a moral fault if the failure to observe them involved a lack of charity.) No doubt one should correct these conventional faults since they can

76

make social life more difficult for those who commit them or have to put up with them. But such faults are usually not a sin and to tell children that they are, can only create difficulties for the proper formation of their conscience.

To avoid creating such difficulties parents need to exercise a very strict control over their own reactions. When they feel the impulse to correct or punish something they feel is wrong in their children, it would always be wise for them to take time off to ask themselves: "But, is this really wrong before God?"

No doubt they will often conclude that it is, because God does not want children to tell lies, or not to learn to control their bad temper, or to be thoughtless about other people (and this includes their obligation to respect their parents' legitimate—though self-sacrificing—right to rest), etc.

But perhaps on other occasions, after having thought it out well, their conclusion will be *No*; because they are prepared to admit that what God does not want is parents who let their nerves get the better of them, or who are too easy on themselves at the same time as they are tyrants over their children, implanting in the home the type of living conditions which simply suit them best. Parents need to be on the lookout for a special type of temptation—which is always lurking along the way of parenthood—which is the temptation to classify as faults in their children things that are really no more than children's natural reaction towards faults in their parents. Parents should keep their minds clear on this point: if something is not wrong before God, however "wrongly" it may be suited to the parents' whims or preferences, then it simply is *not* wrong at all. It should not give rise to angry reactions or punishment, and less still should it be labelled as sinful.

Sin as selfishness

There is another idea that children easily understand and can help them towards a right understanding of sin: the idea that it *is bad to be selfish*. Even among themselves, children quickly recognize selfishness and realize that there is something poor and despicable about this being "out for oneself". This almost instinctive understanding of the mean quality of selfishness can be very useful in helping children understand the badness of sin. Sin is, first and foremost, an offence against God. This is its theological essence. Any theory or explanation of sin which overlooked this essence and presented it simply as some sort of failing on a purely human or social level, would be absolutely deformative. Nevertheless, when teaching children that sin offends God—who is good—one should teach them that it offends him precisely because it is an expression of selfishness; and God does not want us to be selfish, because self-seeking renders our salvation difficult and makes any real happiness, even in this life, impossible. This, then, is his Will and the purpose of his Commandments; to teach us to fight against our self-centered tendencies and help us learn to love.

Children should be taught that there are many ways of offending God by being "out for oneself." There are many forms of selfishness: the selfishness of pride (which is at the root of all other sins, and present in each one of them) the selfishness of lying, greed, covetousness, anger, envy, laziness, sensuality . . . ; the self-seeking, in a word, of each of the capital sins.

Children and mortal sin

Every selfish action, after all, is a sin, even though it may be just a very venial sin. To seek oneself means necessarily to turn one's back on God, however partially. Since experience teaches us that children can be selfish, we should find no difficulty in realizing that they are capable of committing venial sins—which simply means being selfish in little things.

But are children capable of committing mortal sins? Can a ten-year-old child for instance, commit a mortal sin? I think that he can. In fact I think that this conclusion becomes inescapable if one simply asks oneself: are children, who are certainly capable of being selfish in little things, capable of being selfish in big ones? I think that they are. I think that a ten-year-old child is capable of selfishness in a big degree, even to a total degree, i.e. that he is capable of an action by which he centres totally on himself and turns his back completely on God and on others. And that constitutes a mortal sin.

No doubt more than one reader will react at this and will not want to accept such a conclusion. But if he won't accept that a ten-year-old child can commit a mortal sin, then let him say when a child can commit such a sin. At what age would he place the beginning of the capacity of sinning mortally: at age fourteen and not at thirteen? At thirteen, and not at twelve?

It would probably help if we went into this a bit more deeply, and the matter certainly deserves it. A mortal sin is any action which, by centering us completely on ourselves, necessarily breaks our friendship with God. To my mind, a child aged ten is capable of such an action. Think for example of the case of a child who comes to Confession and accuses himself of one of the following: "I deliberately stole one of my brother's things, just to see him fly into a rage", "I hate So-and-So; I'm going to get my own back on him, and I'm not prepared to forgive him", "I did such-and-such, on purpose, so as to make my grand-dad lose his temper"; "I spent the whole week hoping my mother would have an accident and really hurt herself . . . ."

I do not say that these are necessarily grave sins. But it doesn't seem impossible to me, or even very difficult for a sin of this type to cut one's friendship with God, because it can easily imply a gravely self-centered human attitude by which one places one's self at the center of one's own life, looking for self-satisfaction even at the cost of making others suffer. Such an action may therefore easily imply a proud and self-sufficient rejection of loyalty and dependence towards God and other people.

Sin, selfishness and Hell

But—I hear a voice—are you actually suggesting that if a child committed one of these sins and died suddenly, he would go to Hell?

Now this perhaps reveals the real difficulty that we all feel about the idea of mortal sin. If we find it hard to accept the suggestion that a child is capable of sinning mortally, could it be because we find it hard to accept the suggestion that we ourselves are capable of sinning mortally and so meriting Hell? . . .

To clear up this objection, the first thing is to recall that God loves us, that he wants all men to be saved,[1] that he is determined to get us to Heaven. We should therefore get rid of those imaginative ideas about the person who spends a lifetime struggling to behave well but finally has one bad slip and, having the hard luck to die before he can get to Confession, goes to Hell. God, if he can, does not call a person at the wrong moment. He wants to call all of us at a right moment. But it is here that our free will has its part to play, for good or bad. We are capable of making the right moments fewer and fewer and the wrong moments more and more frequent . . . and if we do so we are obviously reducing the possibilities of death overtaking us in a right moment.

Going a little deeper, I would say that while mortal sin does in fact merit Hell, what lands people in Hell in practice is *unrepented* mortal sin.

Even though a person commits many mortal sins, he will be saved if he repents. And (here we link up with our main subject) it should be emphasized that our *conscience*—if it is well formed and if it is followed—is our closest and most intimate ally to help us repent if we have had the misfortune to commit a mortal sin.

God wants to call us at a right moment. And he has so made us that if we offend him seriously by yielding to selfishness in a serious matter, it is hard for us not to realize the fact, because our conscience protests and, deep down inside, we are lacking in peace and happiness until—like the Prodigal Son—we repent and turn back towards our Father God. Conscience exerts a lot of pressure (it is God's grace pressing us through conscience) and the pressure does not ease up until we react and repent. This, please God, is what we normally do, and do quickly, when we sin, But there are many dangers. We may not have a well-formed conscience. We may have got used to not examining it or not obeying it. We may have an insensitive conscience (it is precisely when one does not obey one's conscience that there is the greatest danger of its becoming dulled and insensitive). In such cases, even if we commit grave sins, our repentance can become less immediate, our acts of contrition less frequent, our self-centeredness deeper and more continuous, our attitude of coldness towards God's friendship more deep–rooted, our rejection of his pardon more and more radical. . . .

This is what can happen when a man's conscience does not work well; when he starts telling himself that there is little to worry about in sins that are in fact grave, when he lends a deaf ear to the protests of his conscience, when he does not obey it, when he refuses to repent. It is in this way that a man can fall little by little into total self-centeredness and self-sufficiency; incapable therefore of loving, which means incapable of entering Heaven where only those able to love gain entry.

Continuous rectification

A single act of grave selfishness is not likely to take anyone to Hell. It is the *state* of grave selfishness—the state of obstinate and complete self-centeredness involving the definitive rejection of God's mercy and friendship—that takes people to Hell. A single act of grave selfishness, a single mortal sin, does indeed break one's friendship with God. But if this happens, there is our conscience reproaching us for our conduct, prodding us with its protests, so that we will rectify.

The person who knows how to rectify immediately shows that he has a sensitive conscience. By sinning he separated himself from God. By rectifying he undoes that separation. His rectification may even represent such a step forward that he ends up with a greater degree of love than he possessed before.

What, however, of the person who does not rectify immediately and keeps on postponing his repentance? Such delays are an unmistakable sign that he attaches little importance to the life of grace, to friendship with God. Every day of delayed repentance is a step towards a state where he has lapsed into complete coldness, where his conscience has been definitively silenced, and where there is practically nothing left that could effect a conversion and make the re-birth of grace possible.

That is the state that really threatens man. The danger is all the greater in that one comes to such a state little by little and with relative ease (if one ignores one's conscience); and once one falls into it, it is usually extremely hard to get out again.

We should not find it so difficult, therefore, to realize that any one of us could go to Hell. All that is needed is to forget about one's conscience: refusing to examine it or listen to it or obey it. . . . All that is needed is to develop the facility (which is very easily developed) of finding an excuse for everything one does. All that is needed, in short, is not to face up to the hard and constant work of rectification implied in Christian living. "We must face up to our personal miseries and seek to purify ourselves. . . . The power of God is made manifest in our weakness and it spurs us on to fight, to battle against our defects, although we know that we will never achieve total victory during our pilgrimage on earth. The Christian life is a continuous beginning again each day. It renews itself over and over."[2]

It seems obvious that the best way to avoid attaching too little importance to big sins is to attach the right importance (which will be neither exaggeratedly great nor exaggeratedly small) to little sins. To say the same thing in clearer words, the best way to ensure that one will repent of one's possible mortal sins is to repent of one's actual venial ones. I would therefore assert—in flat contradiction to ideas that are being pressed into circulation today—that to encourage children, from their early years, to confess their sins (which will normally be small sins) frequently in Confession, is a marvellously effective means towards the healthy and balanced formation of their moral conscience. Of course, the reasons that make frequent Confession healthy for little children make it, if anything, healthier still for us adults.

MORAL FORMATION: FURTHER GUIDELINES

The formation of conscience, in the case of children and young people, is a long and continuous process. Proper training given at school will help. Nevertheless, the process should not only be initiated in the home but must be fundamentally carried through there. The following points may guide parents in this continuing task.

The sense of moral duty

It is vital to ensure that the child is little by little acquiring a proper sense of moral duty; that he is gradually grasping why we ought to do certain things and avoid others. . . . One must try to get him to understand that we are not animals; we do not grow automatically; we are not yet stamped with our final make; we can work out well or badly; we are on our way; we can arrive or not; we can be saved or we can be condemned. That is why God, out of love, signposts the way for us. We are obliged to follow his indications if we want to get to our goal which is Heaven. But the obligation we are under is moral *not physical*. God does not physically oblige us to do what he wants, to follow the way that he has sign-posted for us. He leaves us with our freedom. And we are left with the alternatives and consequences of our freedom. We are left with the alternative of either following his indications (because we trust him, because we believe that they are indications given by Truth and Love) or of not following them (because our laziness is reluctant to make the effort they involve, or because our pride is not prepared to accept the Truth or to understand the Love behind them). *But* we are not left with the alternative, if we fail to follow his indications, of not suffering the consequences, for this is not just morally but physically impossible.

If we do not follow his indications—apart from offending him (because we reject an expression of his love)—we will not arrive. Just as a traveller who takes to the road, with the idea of getting to New York, is free to follow the roadsigns or not to follow them. But if he does not follow them, he won't get to New York.

Freedom and responsibility are two basic topics in morality. Moreover they are correlative topics, in such a way that one cannot be considered apart from the other.[3] Since young people today, at least from the age of twelve or thirteen on, are being subjected to growing pressures to understand freedom as the right to do anything without having to think of the consequences or having to bear them, we should try to help them understand that freedom so conceived is not free-dom. It is irresponsibility. Or, if they prefer, it is irresponsible freedom—but this does not mean that one has not got to answer for it. They should realize that responsibility always accompanies freedom. We can forget about it, but we cannot get away from it. Sooner or later it always catches up with us. We will all have to answer for our free actions, and perhaps especially for our irresponsible free actions.

The fact is that young people today (and not only young people) find themselves submerged in an immense fog of confusion surrounding this subject of freedom. It is beyond our scope to consider who or what has caused the fog. But my experience is that people are greatly helped to see through it if they are reminded of an elementary and obvious principle—the principle that if we are free to do this or choose that, we are not free to avoid the *unavoidable* consequences of what in fact we do or choose. . . . I am free to jump out of the twelfth floor window; but if I do, I am not free to avoid the consequence of bashing my head in on the sidewalk. I am free to try drugs, but if I do, I an not free to avoid the consequence of becoming enslaved to them.

Positive reasons

When it comes to specific obligations or prohibitions, parents should always make the effort to explain the positive reasons behind them, the positive objectives they are meant to facilitate.

"You shouldn't do that because it is wrong." This is not a formative "explanation"; it tends rather to deform. It leaves the child with a restrictive and negative idea of morality— which is just the opposite of the idea of Christian morality they should be getting.

"Why do we have to go to Mass?" Not just to fulfil a Commandment (a Commandment is not an end in itself), but *to worship God; to take part together in the sacrifice of Jesus Christ.* One should always underline the *purpose* of the Commandments.

"Why should we pray?" Not just because it is commanded; not even "because that is what every good Christian does ", but in order to learn to talk with God, to get on speaking terms with him.

"Why must we not tell lies?" Because it means misusing the faculty which God has given to us in order to communicate with other people; a lie is a wedge that separates us from God, and from others.

Today's unsettled and confused world presents constant opportunities for clarifying moral standards. Parents should not miss these opportunities offered by newspapers, magazines, television shows, etc., and they should be on the lookout for those that crop up in family conversations.

The moment comes (perhaps not much after the age of ten) when the question "Why can't I see that film or read that book?" is seriously put and has to be seriously answered: "Because it can do you harm", *telling them what that harm is*: it can take away your freedom to love, for purity is a condition of love; it can turn you into a slave of your body. . . .

The task of forming young people's standards in the matter of purity is a particular responsibility of parents. It should be parents who teach their children "gradually about the origins of life, in accordance with their mentality and capacity to understand, gently anticipating their natural curiosity. I consider this very important. There is no reason why children should associate sex with something sinful or find out about something that is in itself noble and holy in a vulgar conversation with a friend. This can also be an important step in strengthening the friendship between parents and children preventing a separation in the early moments of their moral life."[4] It is a task to be fulfilled by stages. But the starting point, and the basic point to be emphasized at all times, is that the differences between the sexes—as well as sexual attraction and sexual union—are part of God's creation. They are God's way to raise up new lives, within marriage, thereby associating man in his creative task. Sex then has something sacred about it, as being particularly related to God's plans for mankind. And sacred things that are specially tied into God's plans, must be also particularly directed to the purpose that God has assigned to them. If this is difficult in the case of sex—because our passions, which are good in themselves, are disordered—then we simply have to learn to control our passions and direct sex to its end. Explanations along these lines will teach children to have a high regard for the virtue of chastity and will make it easier for them, when they begin to run into difficulties to live this virtue *positively* and to look for the support of divine grace in order to strengthen their own human endeavors.

It is essential to begin this work of sex education in good time, without losing sight of two fundamental guidelines:

a) the idea of *reverence* has to be gotten across when dealing with this topic;
b) the idea of reverence has to be gotten across *before the topic becomes a matter of temptation*. Later on may be too late.

Not every restriction limits our freedom

Nevertheless, one should not lose sight of the fact that the first reaction of a young person (and more surprisingly, of many who are not so young) when they come up against a restriction, is to see in it a limitation of their freedom. One should explain to them, time and again, that this is not necessarily so: that not all restrictions necessarily imply a limitation of freedom. It is not hard to get them to understand that energy always needs to be controlled if it is to serve any useful purpose: the energies of a river need to be dammed; the energy of steam needs to be built up inside a boiler; gasoline needs to be compressed and exploded inside a cylinder. Human energies likewise need to be channelled. And if we are meant to apply certain restrictions to them, this is so that we can use these energies throughout our life with greater effect and greater freedom.

One of the simplest and clearest examples to illustrate this point is a road. A road is a restriction. It is a restricted area. It has a limited paved width. It has its curves and its cambers. . . . And if one wants to keep on the road, one has to accept and follow all these restrictions. But they do not limit us: not at least if one understands what a road is for—which is to bring us to a definite destination. And that is what life is for also.

We would be inclined to question the I.Q. of a driver who sets out on a drive with the fixed idea that his driving must be absolutely restriction-less. "Now look at that curve, for instance, that they have just plunked in front of me. I'm not going to stand for it . . . ." If he drove straight on instead of following the curve, this apparent affirmation of his freedom would obviously end him up at the bottom of a ditch or wrapped round the nearest tree.

An expressway makes the example even clearer. It has limited entrance and exit points. It has maximum speed limits and, at times, even minimum speed limits. Nevertheless, no one regards the limitations of an expressway as restrictions of his freedom but rather as factors that favor the most effective use of that freedom.

Training one's will

Children need to be helped to understand that if they have no will power, they will be no good for life. An athlete exercises and trains his muscles so as to be in shape for running. If he didn't train them, his body would let him down. In a similar fashion we have to train our will—exercising the "muscles" of the will by means of little efforts and sacrifices—so as to be in shape for life. A boy or girl who reaches maturity—in terms of age – but with practically no will power, is not mature. They are not fit for life. They could be compared to a ship without a rudder or a car without a steering wheel. The practical side of moral formation is simply aimed at making each one master of his or her own life. This is what the moral *struggle* is about: being in charge—or not—of one's life. It is only by dint of victories—despite some defeats—that one becomes master. And being master means that, with the help of God's grace, a person can take his life where he wants; and not be left drifting, under the control of a thousand things—environment, fashions, friends, passions, laziness—that are not his own proper personality, his own essential *self*.

Defeats

Children need not only to be told—insistently—that life is a struggle. They also need to be told not to be surprised if the struggle turns out to be a hard one, and not to be dismayed if at times they get the worst of it. They will face up to their defeats if we have told them, no less insistently, that God understands us, that he loves us even with our weaknesses, and that he wants to help us. We should therefore have limitless confidence in him. They should be taught to ask him for pardon many times a day (a practice that, far from being burdensome, is a constant reminder that a life lived in God's presence is a life lived in the presence of Love, and that to ask for forgiveness is the reaction of a person in love. The person who stops asking for forgiveness has stopped loving.) They should be taught to make their examination of conscience, very briefly and very simply, each night. And, I repeat, one of the best ways of ensuring that their conscience is being properly formed, without their being saddled with scruples or slipping into laziness, is to encourage them to take up the custom of frequent Confession; from the earliest moment (which should certainly be no later than the age of six or seven) when they are capable of understanding the meaning of offence and the meaning of forgiveness.

Sensitivity to grace

Children, we have said, need a keen awareness not only of the fact that life is a fight, but also of the fact that we are not alone in that fight. They need to acquire a *sensitivity to grace*: to sanctifying grace which makes us children of God; and to actual grace—that help from God which gives light to our minds and strength to our wills so that we keep on fighting and learn to conquer in the fight.

If the father and mother go to Confession and Communion frequently, if they pray, if they visit the Blessed Sacrament, their children will realize that their parents are relying on divine grace to help them in their struggle, and they will learn to do likewise.

Children need to see their parents' example

Parents should give their children clear ideas. But if they want them not only to have a well-formed conscience, but to follow it, then they should not only give them clear ideas, they should also give them clear example. Parents whose children never see them struggling to improve—with ups and downs, but determinedly and with a resilient spirit—will never educate their children well. If the children do not see, for instance, that their father or mother is fighting so as not to give way to nerves—and that they say they are sorry when they fail—then they are not receiving much in the way of example.

An important part of this example lies in the readiness of the parents to impose restrictions on themselves. Children should see that their parents too are prepared to deny themselves things, even though they find them attractive: that their parents can say *No*—also to themselves—even when it is hard. If a mother, for example, wants to form her daughters in a strongly independent attitude towards fashions, she herself must have that same attitude. It is not infrequent to hear mothers complain about how girls today are carried away by fashion or environment. One wonders if those mothers have asked themselves how often *they* have gone against the mainstream of their environment or have said No to the "imperatives" of fashion. . . .

The same goes for fathers. . . (as if fashion didn't influence them too!). If what moves a man when he buys a bigger and more powerful car, is no real family or professional need, but simply the fact that a colleague of his has bought a similar model . . . are his arguments likely to carry much conviction when he tries to persuade his son that a motorcycle is not a "need" for a sixteen-year-old boy?

Parents who want to have children with a sensitive conscience and a strong will, must keep up a constant struggle to acquire these qualities themselves.

Moral decontamination

Here we would do well to give more detailed consideration to the subject of films, books, etc.

If people have the right to expect that the proper authorities will take measures to prevent the streets being littered with refuse, they have a similar right—and the public authorities have a corresponding duty to ensure—that "moral filth" should not be spread around the streets and public places.

How sadly ironic it would be if just as public opinion is waking up to the reality and dangers of environmental contamination, it remained asleep to the infinitely more harmful reality of the moral contamination of our social atmosphere.

If certain individuals wish to poison themselves, in private, that is their business. What is not their business or their right is to claim, in the name of freedom, that poison should be freely sold—or, rather, dearly sold—at every street corner; especially when the poison in question has a particular attraction that makes it peculiarly dangerous.

In certain parts the public authorities are no longer taking any steps to check the moral pollution of our cities and countryside. At time they try to justify their inactivity by the argument that "after all, we haven't any really scientific proof of the harmful effects of pornography, etc." To know the harmful effects of pornography, one doesn't have to wait for the findings of science. One just has to use one's common sense! This, I fear, leaves one doubting the competence of these authorities to govern, for common sense is surely a first requisite for a governor. Of course it may well be that governmental passivity regarding moral contamination is due not so much to a lack of common sense as to the fear of using it, the fear of drawing down on oneself outraged cries of "puritanism", "censorship" etc. which pressure-groups of liberated citizens always manage to orchestrate so effectively. If this is what is paralyzing public authorities then, it is not just common sense that they are lacking, but something much more important: courage—the courage to govern—and a genuine concern for the good of the people.

In all fairness to the authorities it must be said that they would react if they felt that public opinion were in favor of measures of moral decontamination, in favor of the maintenance of certain clear conditions of moral hygiene and cleanliness in public life. But public opinion is mainly made up of parents. And many parents seem to be asleep. Or perhaps, like the authorities we mentioned a moment ago, they are lacking in common sense and courage.

For those who are not asleep, but may be in danger of getting drowsy, here are a few considerations that can help wakefulness.[5]

Self-censorship

Films, television and reading matter have a tremendous influence nowadays on everyone: especially on young people, though also on the not-so-young. Furthermore, it is sadly undeniable that very few modern films or novels do not influence people negatively—especially if one bears in mind that the damage is caused not just by pornographic scenes or passages but by the whole concept of life underlying these works. Materialism is exalted. Pleasure-seeking is the real life-rule. Violence is a positive value; divorce, a sign of civilized progress. Adultery, free love, homosexuality, what-have-you, are to be looked on as something perfectly normal and natural. Film ratings are often very little to go by. An "adult" movie—with its implication that it is *suitable* for "mature" viewers—is usually not suitable for anyone who doesn't want to offend God. A person is mature, in this field, when he is sincere enough to recognize what is degrading and strong enough to avoid it.

Censorship imposed from above may achieve certain results. It may achieve a clean atmosphere in the home or in the street that favors the normal development of a person's affections and passions and avoids the pathetic abnormalities produced by obsession.

But this positive effect will be very limited if it is not accompanied by another achievement—which is to get young people to understand that, in this field, each one of us has to be his own "censor". Clean, happy and free (free also to love): that is how we want to see our young people grow up in this world. And they won't ever grow that way if they don't understand the principle and live the practice of *self-censorship*—which is the only really effective type of censorship that exists. Self-censorship involves a combination of clear ideas and strong will. It means having a clear realization of the damage one can suffer through the obsessing effect of certain shows or literature, or certain ways of behaving. It also means having enough will-power to say *No* to easy slaveries and to fight that difficult but happy fight by which a person defends his freedom, his capacity to love and his soul.

Permissive parents (permissive with their children)

In this matter, just as in all aspects of moral education, it is wise always to try to give positive arguments. Nevertheless, as we said earlier on, one does not easily get children to

91

understand that a restriction or a prohibition can be *positive*. Their reaction, if they are told *No*, is much more likely to be one of protest and resentment, Faced with the pressures created by permissiveness, many parents yield. . . . They yield, thinking perhaps: "because if I don't give way, my children won't obey me. So, either way, they are going to do what they like." Well, I would tell those parents that they have a grave obligation to give clear and firm guidance to their children in these matters, *even though they suspect or are sure their children won't heed them.*

Modern times are hard times, at least for people's souls. Let us take the case of a son or daughter of permissive parents (i.e. weak parents). The boys or girls read or see whatever they want, go wherever they wish, do whatever they feel like. Their parents are worried, and are right to be worried. They talk things over between themselves. But they don't dare to say anything to the boy or girl.

What is the likely result, ten or twenty years later? A ruined life: lost faith, broken marriage, total loneliness. "But . . . surely my parents must have known that I was heading this way? Then, why didn't they try at all costs to stop me?" And to the desolation of a ruined life is added the bitterness of feeling oneself betrayed by one's own parents, the victim of their lack of courage and love.

Take the same case, but let's suppose that the parents do put their foot down, lovingly but firmly. Perhaps the boy or girl doesn't heed them either, and the same result seems predictable—but with one difference. In the midst of the same desolation, the thought can come . . . "My parents realized that this is how I could end up. And they did all they could to stop me. I didn't heed them, but . . . they loved me! My father and my mother loved me!" Such a conviction could be enough to keep a person from final despair. "My parents loved me!" Does it seem small comfort in the midst of a ruined life? It could be sufficient for salvation.

Soft parents (soft with themselves)

In any case many years' experience tells me that if children at times don't obey their parents in these matters, the most frequent reason is that the parents are too soft, not so much with their children, as *with themselves*. They are not prepared to demand of themselves or to deny themselves enough. They are too selfish.

Let us be sincere. The most convincing (and at times the only effective) argument that parents can and should give their children, when telling them they cannot see a particular film or read a particular book, is that *they themselves—the parents —are not going to allow themselves to see or read it either.*

If parents are not ready to impose censorship on themselves whenever it is called for, then their efforts to impose it on their children will necessarily prove deformative.

Let me allow for one particular type of case before proceeding. The themes of certain productions may be sufficiently delicate or complex so as to call for a greater than average degree of experience or of formed criterion, in order to be able to digest them. In such cases, some parents may reasonably feel that their children do not yet possess that criterion or experience, while they do. (Other parents, however, may feel that such works, especially if they are televised, offer a good opportunity to hold a commentated viewing session with their children. The effect then may well be that the parents will enjoy the production less, but their children's outlook will have been more formed and matured.)

Such productions offer no special problem and I am not thinking of them. I am thinking of the thousands of works—on stage, screen and in print—surrounding us today which are becoming more and more filled with the most blatant pornography. It is in relation to these works that parents have to face up to the need for "self-censorship".

Let's not beat about the bush. Pornography means a degrading representation of the sacred reality and the God-given gift of sex. And the person who accepts pornography in his readings or in the shows he sees, offends God gravely, degrades himself and gives a degrading example to others. Such is the case of the person who is not mature enough to apply self-censorship in foreseeable and unforeseen cases. Maturity means avoiding readings or shows that one can reasonably foresee will have a pornographic content. And when one has not had sufficient foresight, maturity means throwing a book aside immediately if one finds pornographic passages in it or getting up and marching out of a show that defrauds one's expectations and turns out to be degrading.

Double moral standards

If parents try to hold on to certain "freedoms" in these matters, which they deny to their children, it is only logical that the children lay a claim to these "freedoms" and determine to win them for themselves in open rebellion or simply behind their parents' backs.

The conclusion is inescapable. There is only one way by which young people can grasp the meaning of true freedom, and learn how it must be lived and how it must be defended, and that is by the example they see in older people—above all and before anyone, in their own parents.

Those parents who are not prepared to live self-censorship in this matter are guilty of appealing to a two-faced moral code. They have two standards of morality: one for themselves and another for their children. They are thus justifying— in their children's eyes—the accusation of hypocrisy which is often hurled by contemporary young people against their elders. And they are practically guaranteeing that their children will neither respect nor obey them.

Facts are facts, and some truths are no less true for being bitter. Parents cannot expect their children to follow the right road if they are determined to travel on the wrong one. They cannot expect their children to be honest, if they are deep in the practice of deceit, especially of self-deception. They cannot expect their children to be strong if they are weak— especially if their weakness is that very special type of weakness that is becoming so common in our contemporary societies: not just the natural weakness of feeling the attraction of impurity (which is a weakness that all of us can feel though we all have the power to resist it), but the unnatural mental and moral weakness of *denying that impurity means degradation and corruption.* Let us add, therefore, that it is not all that clear that modern youth is so wrong in its accusation on this point, because the attitude of a sizeable sector of our contemporary "adult" world really merits no other description than that of *hypocrisy*. Only a hypocrite invokes a double standard of morality: a permissive standard for himself, and a more exacting one for his children. Only the hypocrite presents himself as uncorruptible, which is what is done by anyone who denies he has any selfish tendencies to fight against. Only the hypocrite says he loves his children when by his deliberate example he is destroying them.

But our contemporary teenage world itself—with its tendency to speak and act as if young people too were "incorruptible", as if there were no such thing as sin or personal self-seeking or a conscience that protests or the need to repent and to go to confession—is by no means free from this hypocrisy. It should realize that there is no other name to be given to these attitudes in its case either; and that there is little excuse, for the hypocrite, in having learned his hypocrisy from his elders.

Sincerity in parents

If parents are not sincere, children won't be either. And without sincerity, the whole question of moral struggle is a waste of time. Sincerity is an essential factor in the proper formation of conscience (just as it is a guarantee of its continuing health). Sincerity is so important because it implies acknowledging the truth, "walking in the truth"—even if at times the truth is not as one would have liked. The persons who acknowledge that they have not acted as they would have wished may, with God's grace, end up by attaining their wish. Only the traveller who recognizes he is on the wrong road has any chance of getting back onto the right one.

It is a bad lookout if parents do not manage to get their children to be sincere with them, owning up when they have done something wrong. It is a bad lookout if children lie to their parents. But if it does happen, what should parents do to remedy the situation? *They should be sincere with their children; they should not lie to them!*

At times one has to get cross with children. But it should be crossness without anger. Parents have the obligation (in justice and charity) to correct their children, but without going too far. To get over-cross is to get cross unjustly. Now, if a father or mother gets annoyed unjustly and does not

95

acknowledge the fact (by saying they are sorry), they are being not only unjust but also insincere. He or she realizes that they have been wrong, but does not want to acknowledge it. And that is very like lying.

Children know their parents well. They know them with both their virtues and their defects. Such a deep knowledge is logical and inevitable, as the simple consequence of having shared the same home for so many years. Therefore, any attempt on a father's or mother's part, to hide their defects from their children, is foredoomed to failure. Let us imagine the case of a five-year-old child with an ill-tempered father who does not fight to control his temper, and is not even sincere enough to acknowledge that he has this defect. Perhaps the child does not know that bad temper is a defect, particularly if (as often happens) no one in that home dares to suggest it is. All that the child knows is that it is one of his father's characteristics whose unpleasant effects at times reach him in the form of bellows and blows.

Bad humour, however, breeds bad humour. So the most probable outcome is that the child himself will develop a most awful temper, without knowing how to control it (or even perhaps that it can be controlled) since no one is teaching him how. When the same child has reached the age of fifteen he will almost certainly know that bad temper is a defect, although perhaps, following his father's example, he will not want to admit that it is in his case (there are always excuses!). Total result of this situation: the child will not only have acquired the same defect as his father, but also, in all probability, he will neither respect his father nor love him.

Parents' defects as a formative factor

In the case just given there is a point that should not be overlooked. The basic reason for the child's deformation (and for his consequent lack of love for his father) was not the father's defect, but rather the father's *lack of struggle* against the defect and, above all the father's insincerity as regards the undeniable fact that it was a defect.

What is a cause of deformation (and therefore of scandal) for a boy or girl is not to have parents with defects (for that is inevitable), but to have insincere and hypocritical parents: parents who invariably try to justify or camouflage their defects—under a screen of lies, flare-ups of rage, or abuses of authority—because, when all is said and done, they are just not ready to fight against them.

Their parents' defects should not be a motive of scandal for children, nor even a motive to respect or love them less. None of this will happen if they see that their parents are conscious of those defects, that they acknowledge them and are trying to fight against them. Then the defects of the parents—their sincere fight against their defects—will become a marvellous example and encouragement to the children, to want to do likewise in their own lives. Curiously enough, children tend to have much greater understanding towards their parents when they see them fight against their defects; and so the very parental defects help the children to respect and love their father and mother more.

This can be the last conclusion of this chapter. The way parents look at and tackle their own defects is, humanly speaking, perhaps the factor that most influences their children's moral formation, their growth in sound conscience, and their development of character.

Parents don't need to be geniuses or great psychologists in order to form their children well. They simply need to love them truly, with a love that combines sacrifice, affection and fortitude. They don't need to be saints either—though they should always keep up the hope that, with God's grace, they may in the end yet make it. What they do need is to struggle sincerely to live a Christian life that can be noted in the little things of each day. In words of Msgr Josemaria Escrivá: "Parents teach their children mainly through their own conduct. What a son or daughter looks for in a father or mother is not only a certain amount of knowledge or some more or less effective advice, but primarily something more important: a proof of the value and meaning of life, shown through the life of a specific person, and confirmed in the different situations and circumstances that occur over a period of time.

"If I were to give advice to parents, I would tell them, above all, let your children see that you are trying to live in accordance with your faith. Don't let yourselves be deceived:

they see everything, from their earliest years, and they judge everything. Let them see that God is not only on your lips, but also in your deeds; that you are trying to be loyal and sincere, and that you love each other and you really love them too.

"This is how you will best contribute to making your children become true Christians, men and women of integrity, capable of facing all life's situations with an open spirit."[6]

7   *Ideals in youth*

*"Young people have always had a great
capacity for enthusiasm, for big things, for
high ideals, for everything that is genuine"*
(Msgr Escrivá de Balaguer).

BIG THINGS

The idealism of youth—what an inexhaustible subject!
Psychologists explain it, educators build on it, dema-
gogues exploit it, and (perhaps worse still) older people look
on it with benevolent tolerance or cynical scepticism, and
wink knowingly to one another: "they'll learn."

Young people certainly will learn many things from their
elders and from the way they live. Hopefully, one of the
things they will not learn is cynicism, i.e. the loss of their
ideals. Whether this occurs or not depends largely on the type
of older person they happen to meet.

If an older person takes it for granted that, though it is
logical that young people have ideals, it is also logical and
besides inevitable that they end up by losing them, then one
can only conclude that the older person in question either
does not believe much in ideals, or else does not believe much
in young people.

If a parent wants a self-assessment as to how he stands on
this point, he would do well to quiz himself with a few
questions such as:

"Do I believe in the idealism of young people? Do I believe
that their hearts are made for big things?"

"Do I—who have to bring them up—believe in big things?"

"Are the big things I believe in big enough for their
ideals?"

Only the person who can answer each of these questions
affirmatively can entertain some hope of being a good parent.

Ideals in constant growth

One of the many striking things about Msgr Josemaria Escrivá was his belief that young people need never lose the ideals of their youth. He rather believed that these ideals could and should grow indefinitely. He had his own experience to go by; his personal ideals grew steadily from the age of fifteen to his death almost sixty years later. And he could also go by his experience with millions of young people from all over the world.

Msgr Escrivá was a firm believer in the idealism of the young (and the not so young). But, being a realist and—above all—a man of faith, he knew that the human heart was made not just for any ideals, but only for the ideals that Christ brought to earth. He knew that these are the only ideals capable of filling our hearts—to overflowing—during a lifetime. His own life was entirely devoted to incarnating these ideals and awakening them in others.

Msgr Escrivá, I have just said, was a realist. By this I also mean that he was perfectly well aware that a young person's heart is not just a focal-point of ideals; it is a field of battle. He addressed his message to all. But his insistence that we are called to the highest possible ideals was constantly accompanied by the reminder that we are all equally capable of the greatest possible crimes, and must therefore be prepared for a life-long struggle. Now, if the struggle hits all of us, it obviously hits harder when it hits first—which is in adolescence. Let us take a closer look at those early teen years when a boy or a girl is no longer a child but is not yet a man or a woman either, and stands therefore in special need of his or her parents' understanding.

The age of contrasts

It is the age of contrasts. Life, in youth, seems bigger. It seems to offer more. It is filled with the challenge of great things. And the young person feels ready to take up the challenge. But life, in youth, also seems more complicated; and the young person finds him or herself faced with new difficulties or with old ones that have suddenly grown worse: selfishness, sensuality, laziness, rebelliousness. . . . It is the age of contrasts: nobleness on the one hand; calculation on the other. It is the age of enthusiastic victories and of discouraging defeats. It is, or should be, the age of struggle. The point is well expressed in the following words of Msgr Escrivá, speaking to a group of young people in October, 1972: "You can't give up fighting, because our life is just one continuous tug-of-war. The craziest things attract us. It's humiliating, isn't it? St Augustine used to say that his passions were constantly trying to pull him to the ground, But at the same time, along with these crazy ideas, we feel a great urge to do something worthwhile, to serve other people, to live a pure life, to work in things that can help others, to sacrifice ourselves. Isn't that true too? And it is then that the struggle breaks out between our passions seeking to pull us down, and those other wonderful longings, that spur us upwards. We have got to fight. There's just no alternative."

It is elementary for a parent to realise that adolescence marks the outbreak of this war between high-mindedness and calculation.

It is also obvious and elementary to realise (and I suppose that practically everyone realizes it) that there could be fewer proofs more decisive of being a poor parent than the readiness to spoil children by giving them whatever they ask, or allowing them whatever they want. The grown-up person who acts in this way turns himself into the accomplice of a young person's selfishness; he becomes the ally of his mean and calculating instincts, and so practically guarantees the defeat of that young person's idealism and the destruction of his generosity and capacity for sacrifice.

It ought to be no less obvious and no less elementary to realize (and, nevertheless, my impression is that many parents do not realize it) that one can prove oneself to be a bad parent by falling into another error: a subtler (but perhaps more harmful) error, which is to let the great and noble ideals of youth be edged out and replaced by limited and calculated objectives: narrow and selfish objectives which, even if at times they leave little room for laziness, always leave plenty for individualism and self-centredness; and which, whatever else they may give if achieved, cannot give happiness. Let me try to explain what I am getting at.

An ideal is something great. It is essentially felt to be something greater than one's self. It is something which, by the sheer force of its beauty and nobility, makes a person want to get away from himself, to forget himself, so as to defend, to admire, to love and serve that ideal, and strive upwards towards it. A person with an ideal is ready to live for it and if necessary, even to die for it. There are not all that many true ideals: love, family, country, God. . . .

An objective, in contrast, is something—felt to be of worth—that one hopes to gain and make one's own. It may be something difficult to attain. It may be something great. But it is seldom, if ever, seen as being greater than one's own self (if so seen it would tend to turn into an ideal, to be served; or into a humiliating irritant, to be rejected or hated). An objective attracts because it promises to satisfy some specific personal desire: the desire for power or pleasure or popularity, or the simple desire to progress and improve oneself. . . . There lies its worth.

An objective is something that can be conquered (an ideal, never). A man should always have objectives before him because he needs always to keep moving ahead. But if he attains his objectives there are different ways in which he can use them. He can use them as a support under his feet, as a springboard to help him reach closer to his ideal (which is still far off). Or he can just stay put, smugly looking at what he has attained, as if there was nothing more left for him to achieve. He is so proud of having achieved his objectives that he forgets his ideal, if in fact he ever had one.

A person who has ideals will always have objectives. But some people have objectives without having ideals. If a man dreams of an ideal love, of an ideal woman, and thinks he has found her, he falls in love. . . . His objective then will be to marry her. If they get married, he will have achieved his objective. But (if his love is real) she will continue to be his ideal and he will realize that despite all his efforts to achieve other objectives (to keep improving in points of character, for instance), he will never be worthy of her. It would be sad if he ever came to feel he was at last worthy of her, and worse still if he ever felt her to be unworthy of him. Idealism would have collapsed in that marriage.[1]

The man who wants to marry for money, has an objective but not an ideal. If he succeeds in marrying a rich heiress or a widow with a million, he has attained his objective. And that is as far as he wanted to go. Ideals just did not enter into his plans.

A boy with no objectives is (or will turn out to be) a lazy boy. Anyone can see that. But a boy with no ideals is and will always be a disaster—no matter how many objectives he has and what efforts he makes to attain them. The sad thing is that lots of parents don't see this, though it is parents who should be their children's main guides. They don't seem to realize that the objectives-without-ideals formula for life can turn out energetic people perhaps, but not happy people. For a life without ideals can only be selfish and vain, and therefore unhappy.

There are far too many parents around who (in relation to their children and even at times in relation to themselves) cannot see the difference between high ideals and self-centred aims; between ideals that ennoble a person's character., and aims that (unless they are directed towards a higher end, a true ideal) diminish it. And so they allow or even cause the noble ideals of adolescence to be debased and turned aside into poor and inadequate objectives.

One sees so many cases! Parents with a fairly bright son or daughter who constantly push him or her to come out number one in their class. And the young person ends up quite centered on that goal and quite satisfied if they attain it. It is a very bad thing indeed to be satisfied in youth. One can think of plenty of other cases. the father with an athletic son who provides him with every sort of stimulus (clubs, coaches, trips) and so manages to turn out a boy whose one aim is to become a tennis or swimming champion. Or the mother who allows (or perhaps again encourages) her teenage daughter to think that the one thing that really matters in life is to be popular with boys and so she has no thoughts in her pretty little head except for clothes and other ways of attracting their attention.

What's wrong with wanting to be a tennis champion?

"Now, just a moment," I hear an objection, "are you really suggesting that young people with brains shouldn't work to get good marks, or that kids with the making of tennis champions should not try to make it, or that girls shouldn't like making themselves up and looking attractive?" No; I am not making any such suggestions. It seems to me quite natural that young people do all of these things. What I am suggesting, however, is that they should not be led or allowed to believe that, in doing them, they are striving for ideals. They are striving for aims or objectives which, I repeat, is not the same thing. What I would like to emphasize is that the teenage boy or girl who simply fills their life with these things is leaving it empty of ideals. And a life empty of ideals is heading for unhappiness. It is a tremendous pity if children or parents fool themselves on this point. It is sadder still if parents are to blame for having deceived their children on the matter.

Isn't it true that the roads along which far too many parents seem to be pushing their children are roads of selfishness, silly vanity or narrow ambition? But why? Why have these parents been such poor pupils in the school of life? How is it that they are so unconcerned to spare their children, if they can, the mistakes that stand out in their own experience?

Proud of their parents?

Later on in life, are such children likely to be proud of their parents or to be content with themselves? Are they likely to be proud of their parents later on ? I don't know. I do know of boys or girls who have later on (rightly or wrongly) come to the conclusion that their parents' concern to see them "tops" in studies or sports or popularity, was due more to the father's or mother's vanity than to a genuine respect for the young person's distinctive personality or to a more mature and deeper understanding (such as might be expected of a grown-up person) of the qualities that go to make up true happiness. (After all, one of the elementary facts of family psychology is that a parent's determination to see a son or daughter come out on top is at times the unconscious reflection of the parent's desire to compensate for the failures they themselves experienced in *their own* youth.)

Are such children likely to be content with themselves if, say twenty or thirty years later, they sit down to a sincere self-examination and find themselves lacking in ideals? I doubt it. Are they not rather likely to go through something similar to the experience Julien Green narrates in his *Journal*? At the age of forty two, he takes a long look back, and out of his memories he fashions a dialogue with his own self of twenty five year ago. Rather than a dialogue, one would have to call it a sort of cross-examination to which his far-away youth, brimful of ideals, submits the miserable and impoverished reality which marks the sum total of his mature years: "You have cheated me. You have robbed me. Where are all those dreams I entrusted to you? What have you done with all of that richness I was fool enough to place in your hands? I answered for you, I was your guarantor; and you have gone bankrupt on me. I should have run away with all that was still in my possession and which you have since squandered. Far from admiring you, I despise you." And Green adds: "And what would the older of the two allege in his self-defence? He would speak of all the experience he had acquired. He would talk of his solid reputation. He would turn out his pockets, and look desperately through the drawers of his writing-desk for something to justify his life by. But he would make a bad job of his defence, and I think he would feel thoroughly ashamed of himself."[2]

IDEALS AND MODELS

Human heroes

Young people seldom get enthusiastic about abstract ideals. But they are easily attracted by the ideal or idealized persons or personages that they meet in real life, or that are conjured up before them in fiction (novels, films, etc.). With this in mind, the following points may be useful:

—our modern world is so commercialized and so dominated by public relations, that it is often difficult to distinguish between what is real and what is fictitious. It is no exaggeration to say that the image presented to us of many real persons (pop-singers, film-stars, sports figures, racing-car drivers. . .) is largely composed of fiction;

—the fictitious version of the life of a *real* person can exercise greater influence (and, if the "values" it offers are negative, it can do greater harm) than the presentation of the life of a fictitious person (for instance, a character in a television series), because the reader or viewer *knows* that the latter is fictitious, and he may *think* that the former is real. . . ;

—generally speaking, the heroes of modern novels, etc. possess less human virtues than the heroes of the popular novels or stories of thirty or fifty years ago. Modern 'heroes', in fact, are often presented with a whole string of anti-hero characteristics; apart from their bravery (which at times is hardly distinguishable from the recklessness of a person who simply looks contemptuously on life), they are frequently cruel, unscrupulous, untrusting, untrustworthy, sexually promiscuous, selfish, superficial, inconstant and vain. . . ;

—those parents who see the seriousness of this last point would do well to try to develop—in their teenage children (ten-twelve years old)—a taste for the great adventure stories of fiction (Jules Verne type) or for the real-life accounts of geographical exploration, scientific discovery, mountain or space conquest, etc. In this way they will familiarise them with the real details—the ups and downs, the hopes and disappointments, the suffering and endurance—of true-to-life heroes. It is better if a boy's sense of hero-worship is stirred by the life and adventures of an Arctic explorer or a Himalayan mountain climber than by that of a football star or someone out of contemporary show-business. Are girls more easily captivated by the tinsel glamour surrounding stars, models, pop-stars, etc.? Perhaps; and if so, it is undoubtedly harder to enthuse them with valid and healthy heroes and heroines drawn from real life. There is a special challenge here for script-writers, novelists, etc. prepared to devote their talents to the task of creating or presenting, in literary, artistic or journalistic form, figures capable of awakening a nobler and deeper admiration among girls.[3]

Parents as their children's ideal?

Every father, and every mother, must strive to be in some way, if not their children's ideal, at least a model for them; or rather perhaps a copy of the model. For the model and the ideal, as we will see shortly, is Someone else. But a copy, even if it is a poor copy, can get across some idea of the original.

It should be clear however that a parent ought not to try to be his or her children's ideal. He won't make the grade. He's just not up to it. The parent who sets out to be his or her son's or daughter's ideal, would be setting himself or herself up as an idol, as a false god. And when the let-down comes for the children (and it will come), it can turn out to be pretty costly: costly for the parent, costly for the children, and costly for the proper parent-children relationship that should exist between them.

There is an age at which many children tend to "idolize" their parents, especially their father (perhaps mothers are too close to them, or too sensible, to allow it). For as long as it lasts, this idolatry may flatter a father's vanity. His common sense, however, as well as his sense of loyalty towards his children, should make him ensure that it lasts the shortest time possible. He should be the first to stick a pin into that bubble-self and burst the false ideal, before life itself bursts it. If a boy sees that his father plays tennis much better that he does and begins to think that he plays it better than anyone, then his father should disabuse him in a hurry by the simple process of showing him a real champion. Or if the kid thinks that his dad must be the world's number one expert in physics or astronomy, then he might send him to an encyclo-paedia to look up a few Nobel Prize winners. . . .

The temptation of wanting to play god in one's own home is an absurd temptation. Yet quite a few parents toy around with it for a time. Silly parents. The sensible ones step down from the pedestal as soon as possible. Sensible parents don't go round making a show of their limitations, defects or mistakes. But they don't act the hypocrite either, trying to cover them up before their children. What good this sincerity on the parents' part does to the children! It teaches them that their parents are not self-satisfied or self-centered, but are living for a higher ideal.

Christ is the ideal

Parents and teachers therefore have to be constantly on the alert so as not to adulterate young people's idealism with false ideals or unworthy idols, or let it be sidetracked into self-centered aims that only tend to make a person selfishly unhappy or consciously frustrated. What then are the genuine ideals that should be put before young people?

Christian ideals, of course. Or, to be more precise, *the* christian ideal—which is Christ. If Christ really and truly becomes *the ideal* of a person, then all his or her other true human ideals will become centered on Him, and so will find support and stimulus and purification. Without Christ at the center, all the other human ideals die away.

I wonder if this idea, that Christ should be the young person's ideal, seems surprising or insufficient or impractical. If it does, this is surely a sign of the extent to which we have *depersonalized* our religion, making it cold and lifeless. Is it not possible that we have reduced our religion to a sort of business transaction—getting to Heaven in exchange for observing certain rules and living within a system—when it should rather be a matter of fulfilling these rules *because we love a Person*, because we love Jesus Christ (and though Him, the Father and the Holy Spirit)? Surely it is in this way, as a Love-affair, that we should see our religion? A Love-affair which here on earth—where we are constantly seeking and finding Our Lord, getting to know Him, returning to Him whenever we fail Him, learning to serve Him, introducing Him to others— is like a prolonged but enthusiastic courtship that will reach its consummation, its full and glorious union, in Eternity.

If, despite everything, the Person of Christ regarded as the ideal that our young people (and we ourselves) need, still seemed to us too theoretical or out-of-this-world to be a practical proposition, this would be clear proof of our own

108

lack of acquaintance and friendship with Him. A little thought should help us realize where we have gone wrong.

Do we doubt that Christ can really attract the young people of our day? How little we know Him! And how little we know them! We can far too readily dismiss things like the "Jesus Movements" as emotional flashes-in-the-pan, and fail to see the important message they contain: that many young people, including quite a few who reject what they term institutionalized religions, feel themselves strongly attracted by the most elementary human knowledge of the figure of Jesus.

Yes, but what would happen if they knew Him better? Some would undoubtedly abandon their enthusiasm because the real Jesus is demanding, for He is God. But many others—who have a greater instinct of generosity and realize in their hearts that any worthwhile ideal involves sacrifice—would come to Him because Jesus Christ, demanding as He is and all, attracts.

Even on the purely natural level, the good parent or educator realizes that the native idealism of youth is a sign that young people know they are made for bigger things and are somehow restless if they cannot rise to them. For the Christian parent or educator, this idealism should be the springboard from which the young person can reach up to Christ. Perhaps the task cannot be expressed more concisely than in the formula constantly repeated by Msgr Escrivá—to educate children in such a way that, from their earliest days or in full adolescence, their hearts beat to the ideal of seeking Christ, of meeting and getting to know Him, of following Him, loving Him and remaining with Him.

CHRIST AS THE IDEAL

What does it mean in practice to have Christ as one's ideal? I would suggest four main things:

1. to be *friends with* Christ
2. to be *loyal to* Christ
3. to be *proud of* Christ; and (as a consequence)
4. to want to *introduce Christ to others*.

Let us see what each of these four headings may imply, and how parents or the family can help in realizing them.

109

1. *Friends with Christ*

Young people are hero-worshippers by nature. They find their heroes or heroines in fiction, and in real life too. There is scarcely a boy or a girl who has not got their star. They admire them. They read their biographies. They get excited at the mere possibility of seeing them. And all of this is true, even though they normally have to admire their heroes from a distance, probably without the chance of ever speaking with them, much less of becoming friends of theirs.

And are we then going to suggest that Jesus Christ—perfect God and perfect Man—is not capable of attracting them? If they want a Superstar, there is Jesus. Not a poor stage parody, but the tremendous reality of the God-Man who lays down His life out of love for each one of us.

But if one is not constantly reading the life of Jesus, how can one get to know and love Him each day more and more? If someone answers, "Oh, you mean the Gospel? Why, I've read it already. I know what it's all about", he should be told, "No! you don't get to know the life of God become Man in a single reading, nor in a thousand. Keep reading the Gospel, and you'll find that you always get more out of it; you always get to know Him better; He always attracts you more."

Besides, that Jesus, who is so wonderful, *lives*. You can talk with Him. And there we have prayer (which means conversation with the Friend) as another main means for striking up friendship.[4] Five minutes each day, using your own words, full of faith, realizing that He is looking at you, listening to you, understanding and loving you. We need to talk and listen to Him in our prayer. And we need to receive and be fed by Him in the Eucharist. To receive the Eucharist means to let God Himself "work" inside us, communicating His very life to us and strengthening our faith and our love.

Is it hard to get a young person to see all this? I don't think so. But it will mainly depend on what the boy or girl sees and senses in their own family. The parents may be "practising" Catholics, they may even be exemplary parishioners and so on, but. . . if the youngster does not acquire the growing conviction that religion, for his parents, means above all a personal friendship—with a Friend with whom *he* is not yet so friendly—then his ambition to seek that friendship is not likely to be stirred.

110

It is so very different if children begin to realize that when their parents pray, they are really talking with God. Again, few religion classes can teach children as much about what the Eucharist should mean as the simple sight of their parents staying on for a few minutes thanksgiving after Holy Communion—and obviously relishing those moments of special intimacy with Our Lord.

A family needs to pray together, though it is wise if the children's part in family prayers is as voluntary as possible. But is it not likely that they would be keener to take part in the Rosary, for example, if they were taught that this devotion is closely connected with the Gospel: that it is, in words of Pope Paul VI, a way of contemplating "the mysteries—the deeds—of the life of Christ seen through the Heart of Her who was closest to Our Lord."[5]

2. *Loyal to Christ*

In the second place, we said, there must be loyalty towards Christ. The more friendship there is, the easier it is to be loyal. Nevertheless, it is wise to emphasize that forgiveness has an essential role within friendship: forgiving, on the one hand, which is something that Our Lord, who is God, is tireless in doing with us; and asking to be forgiven, which is something that we who are human and very often offend Him, should learn to ask of Him.

A first expression of loyalty, therefore, is *repentance* immediately after a fault, and if needed, *confession*. This is simply the process by which love is born again. It is necessary, then, to insist on how important it is that children see their parents go to Confession frequently?

Since there is so much talk today, especially among young people, about freedom, it is good to remind them that freedom means our ability to say Yes *or* No; that each time we say Yes to something, we say No to other things. What matters therefore, is not to be able to say Yes to oneself, as if being a Yes-man to self were a sign of a well-developed or a well-defended personality. When all is said and done, to say Yes to oneself generally means saying yes to one's selfishness—which is a sign not of personality but of weakness and self-

111

indulgence. For a true personality, what matters is the ability to say Yes to other people, in all of the noble demands which our life with them involves. What matters above all is to be able to say Yes to God, for that is what love for Him means; and to continue saying Yes, even when it is hard, for that is what loyalty to Him means.

It can be so helpful to young persons if they are taught that these are the alternatives involved in any moral problem: being loyal, or being disloyal, to Christ! It helps them so much if they are told that life for all of us is the up-and-down story of how we now choose one alternative, and then perhaps the other, And that salvation means having more ups than downs, cancelling out our acts of disloyalty by acts of loyalty.

3. *Proud of Christ*

"You have to learn how to live a Christian life in a pagan atmosphere", I tell young people time and again. It is true because, to all practical intents and purposes, the social and moral atmosphere surrounding us all today is pagan. It is never easy to go against the social grain or cut across current fashions. And a person can find himself strongly tempted to yield, to keep quiet, to hide the fact that he is a Christian, out of fear of what people may say. He may be tempted, in a word, to be ashamed of his faith, which is the same as being ashamed of Christ.

St Paul, in another period of paganism, felt this temptation, or at least realized that it could hit his fellow-Christians. And so he encouraged them, saying in his usual forceful way, "I am not ashamed of the Gospel!"[6] St Paul had not lived with Christ during the years of Our Lord's life on earth. But he had gotten to know Him so well through prayer and the contemplation of all the details he had been able to learn from others about Jesus (details that we too can learn in the Gospel). He well remembered those words of Our Lord, "If anyone is ashamed of me and of my doctrine before this sinful and adulterous generation, the Son of Man will also be ashamed of him when he comes."[7] He was ashamed neither of Christ nor of His doctrine. He felt happy and proud to follow Him. If we

112

help our young people to get to know Christ, they will easily feel the same healthy and holy pride in following Him.

Let us list a few expressions of this holy pride. A Christian should feel proud of Christ's friendship, proud of Christ's teaching, proud of Christ's example.

Proud of Christ's friendship —This is how the Christian should feel: proud of the friendship which Christ has for him. And proud of the expressions of friendship towards Our Lord he himself wants to show. Proud, therefore, of his piety—which simply means the devout fulfilment of his religious practices. For example, he will not be ashamed to go to Mass, or to have others notice that he is trying to follow the Mass well without yielding to distractions. He will not be ashamed to say the Angelus, or to make a visit to the Blessed Sacrament, even when the friends he is with raise their eyebrows. And he will live these expressions of piety without any fear of being accused of "holier-than-thou" attitudes—because he knows he is simply living out what he has good reason to be proud of. Like the son who feels proud of his parents or his brothers and sisters. When he is away from home, studying or working, he is not in the least concerned if his companions realize that he writes or phones them or buys them presents.

Proud of Christ's teaching —Because it is a teaching that sets people free. "You will know the truth", Jesus said, "and the truth will make you free."[8]

In a world increasingly controlled by hatred, selfishness and runaway passions, it should not be difficult (it is not, in my experience) to arouse young people's enthusiasm for the human nobility of Christian living. Let us remind them of these words of Msgr Escrivá: "We have to act in such a way that those who see us can say: this man is a Christian, because he does not hate, because he is willing to understand, because he is not a fanatic, because he can control his instincts, because he is ready to make sacrifices, because he shows he is a man of peace, because he knows how to love." Let us explain to them that this program is based on a real and constant rebellion, the greatest rebellion, Msgr Escrivá used always to say, that any person can get involved in, and the only one that is

113

really worthwhile: the rebellion of each one of us against his or her own selfishness.

I would like to emphasize this point. If, for example, you speak to them clearly and positively about purity, my experience is that young people have no difficulty in seeing through the pathetic hypocrisy of those who would dismiss all restraint in sexual matters as a sign of a Victorian hangover. They understand that those who take this line, far from being more liberated or mature, are in fact weaker and more enslaved, and above all incapable of really loving. And, again in a phrase of the Founder of Opus Dei, they realize that purity is a "joyful affirmation"; that it is a condition of freedom, of grace, of love; and that the person who understands what love is about is happy to face up to the struggle needed for purity.

In the case of girls this can be especially important, It is obviously only by doing violence to her own womanly nature that a girl or a woman can throw her inborn and deeply-rooted feminine modesty on the dust-heap. When, in spite of everything, she does so—as quite a number to today—the logical consequence is that men cease to respect her. They may ogle at her, but they do not admire her. Their looks express desire; they express anything but respect. After all, what a man who is really a man and not just a human animal looks for in a woman is something more than mere physical attractions. He looks for delicacy, grace, tenderness, sensitivity, understanding, personality, reserve and modesty. These are qualities he can admire. If he doesn't find them, his admiration for the woman's physical attractions will degenerate into mere desire, and his attitude towards her as a person, into contempt.

Is it so hard for a girl to realize there is a big difference between being looked at and being admired? Or that if, by her way of behaving or dressing, she draws men to desire her in a specific way, she is not making herself respected by them, she is making herself despised? A mother who really loves her daughter should have no difficulty in getting these points across to her. Provided she backs up her words with her own example, a mother should have no difficulty in explaining to her daughter that modesty in a woman is simply the expres-

114

sion of her determination to be treated as a person and not as an object.

These reflections should help us to appreciate once more the marvel of Christian morality, as we see how it is both a support and a defence of human values. How could anyone not be proud of moral standards which are the very basis for human nobleness itself?

It is clear that the truth of Christ, which makes us free, does not refer only to the sphere of sexuality. Do we not also feel proud of Christ's doctrine which makes us know ourselves and helps us to overcome fear as we acknowledge ourselves as sinners? So it helps us avoid falling into the isolation of pride. It makes us humble, open and understanding with others.

And we feel proud of the doctrine of Christ which teaches us that the world is good—as a means, not as an end in itself. It sets us on our guard, therefore, against the temptations of all those false philosophies that are forever promising man a hedonist, materialist or Marxist paradise here on earth. Christ's doctrine, by teaching us that our real and lasting treasure lies in Heaven with Him, and by encouraging us to put our hearts there also, helps us precisely to be more detached, less envious and covetous and so enables us to be more truly concerned for the well-being and material welfare of others.

No one should outdo the Christian in his concern for other people. This too is part of what his ideal, Christ, teaches him.

Proud of Christ's example   —This is why I said the Christian should feel proud of Christ's example. He should feel proud of the way Christ gave himself to others. And he should feel proud too of the ways in which he himself can imitate that example of dedication and service. As he tries to fulfil Christ's New Commandment of mutual love—"by this all men will know that you are my disciples, if you have love for one another"[9]—he should remember those other words of Our Lord: "the Son of Man has not come to be served, but to serve." [10]

To serve other people: what a great ideal! And how seldom met today. There are contexts in which the word is used—

115

servants, domestic service—which frankly tend to put-off many people today. Nevertheless, when all is said and done, it remains an ideal that has a powerful attraction for the young people of our times. That this is so true, is borne out by the voluntary youth services that abound today as never before: work-camps, dispensaries, rural schools, and so on.

The most common and perhaps the most wonderful example of service, for love's sake, is that of mothers in their dedication to the home. If each son and daughter is assigned a family-task, it is easy to get them to understand that to fulfil their job well is a way of serving others, a way of loving them. When, despite everything, they get cross at times, because they find their job hard, that is precisely the best opportunity to teach them that, true enough, love at times is difficult, but that these inevitable difficulties need not take away the smile that can always accompany love and service. If parents in their dedication to their family, smile always (or almost always), they are turning their home into a marvellous school of Christian spirit and idealism.

Service as an ideal   At times, however, one meets Christian mothers who sacrifice themselves unstintingly in their dedication to their families, but who seem incapable of appreciating, and certainly do not encourage, the various ways in which their daughters seek to give outlet to their noble instincts for service. They are anything but enthusiastic if one of their daughters wants to train for nursing. They get scared if another is keen on studying domestic science. They accept a proposal to become a teacher—but, oh so reluctantly! . . . Just as well that the girl's instincts in such cases are usually healthier than their mothers' prejudices.

Some professions obviously call more particularly for a spirit of service, and it is important to help young people appreciate this aspect of such a career if they intend to take it up. Medicine no doubt stands out, as perhaps the noblest of all human professions. Nevertheless, we are in a moment when the very nature of Medicine is being threatened by anti-life movements (abortion, sterilization, contraception, euthanasia). There is an urgent need for a reevaluation of the true meaning of the medical profession as a profession at the service of life. Doctors can do so much here by taking part in professional orientation courses, etc., they can communicate genuine and noble professional ideals to young people who mean to become doctors or nurses.

Let us turn to military service. In countries where it is obligatory, this may undoubtedly make it more difficult for people to appreciate its noble qualities of service towards one's native land. Yet, one could scarcely over-emphasize how important it is that a spirit of disinterested service should be maintained and grow in the armed forces.

And what about public service? What about politics as a service-profession? Politics is perhaps the most important profession, and is often the least Christianized. By Christian politics, I am not of course referring to leftist or rightist politics, but simply to a political philosophy and political practice of *service* to the common welfare. Politics is indeed a noble profession when politicians cherish the ideal of service and, if they are in authority, use their authority in order to serve.

Is this hard to achieve? Yes, it is. Is it utopian or impossible? Not at all. To think that it can never be achieved would be to show an unjustified lack of trust in the idealism of our young people who will be tomorrow's politicians. It would amount to saying that a power grabbing spirit—wanting positions of authority simply so as to be one of the top dogs—must necessarily prevail over selflessness, loyalty and nobility. Why should we think so? We have no right to yield to such a pessimistic view, to such a philosophy of determinism. We should rather firmly believe that, if the love of Christ is kept before our young people's eyes, they will be better servants than anyone of the common good.

In short, we should go over each of the professions so as to pinpoint and emphasize its aspect of service towards others and towards society. And at the same time we should point out how the Christian who wants to imitate Jesus Christ has more motives than anyone so as to turn a generous desire to serve into the real inspiration of his professional work.

The ideal in study Perhaps we might finish this section by referring more specifically to the theme of study. Few adolescents are "book worms" by nature. Most of them find study hard. And since, if they do not study, they will not mature for life nor even be able to earn their living, we seem clearly bound to push them to study.

True. Though perhaps to "push" them is not the best way to put it. The results of pushing generally don't last very long. You can push a car with its engine switched off and it will move. But once you stop pushing, the car stops too. What you really have to do is to get the engine working, and then the car will go by itself. Pushing can help in this, but not if the ignition is not connected. . . . Something similar happens with young people's studies. Threats of punishment, the prospect of having to spend the holidays over one's books, the help a tutor can give through private classes . . . such things can give them a temporary push. But none of it gets to the heart of the problem. And as soon as the immediate pressure is over, laziness returns and the boy's or girl's studies begin to drag again. And there they are, grinding along in first gear, way below capacity.

What matters with young students is not so much to push them from outside as to get them to move themselves from within. The key lies in *motivating* them. This is what sets them going.

But I would emphasize that the motivations put before them should be serious and lasting; and if possible, noble. From what I said at the start it should be clear that the promise of rewards or prizes is not a good motivation. Neither is it enough to threaten or encourage them with ideas such as, "if you don't learn to study you'll never be a man", "if you don't study, you'll never get through university, you'll never be able to raise a family. . . ." This is not enough. What should move them to study, already from these early years, must be their *ideals*.

The main motive to put before them is that of pleasing God. God wants each one of us to fulfil the specific duties of his or her state. The student's job, his God-given job, is to study. When he does so, therefore, he is carrying out God's will, This is a fact he should be *consciously* aware of. It will help him if he studies with a small crucifix before him, placed on his study-table or on the pages of his textbook. He should study out of *love*, in order to please the God he loves. In this way he can discover that an hour of study, instead of being a sort of martyrdom, or at least a colossal bore, can be an hour of friendship: "an hour of prayer".[11]

An apostolic motive should also inspire him in his study. The boy or girl should know that they can offer each study period for others. But it is also important for them to realize that by studying properly today, they are laying the foundation for an important work tomorrow. They are qualifying themselves so that they can become someone on whom God can rely later on: in their university years, when they set up a family, in their professional life; so that their solidly acquired professional prestige and their spirit of service towards others will help bring Christ into the most varied human activities, along with all the noble values and ideals that His presence inspires.

4. Longing to introduce Christ to others

Young people formed in this way will not be on the defensive about their Christianity. Proud of Christ and proud of all that he asks of them for their good and the good of mankind, they will want to make him known, to spread faith in him, to share the joy that becoming friends with him and following him bring. In other words, they will do *apostolate*. This should not imply an impertinent interference in the lives of others, or a failure to respect other people's freedom or rights. It should simply mean stirring them with the example of a cheerful, clean and generous way of living, and so waking them to the great and beautiful things that can be discovered in life.

Msgr Escrivá used often to say that Christians in the world should act with a "superiority complex". This implies no contemptuous attitude towards others. Quite the contrary! It implies a desire to see them open their eyes, look upwards and see the "magnalia Dei"—God's wonders which we, despite our defects and unfaithfulness and by His mercy, know and see.

I remember the old joke in England about the difference between the Cambridge graduate and the Oxford graduate. The Cambridge man gives the impression of being the owner of the world, while the Oxford man gives the impression of not caring two hoots who owns the world. . . . I've always felt like adding, in all earnestness, that we Christians should give the impression of knowing *Who* owns the world: my father—who is God. I know that he is my father and that I am his child and heir. So many others around me who are or can be children and heirs of God, do not seem to know it. Let's give them a good awakening!

AND OTHER PEOPLE?

There is a further question that we might ask about the young Christian who is trying to live out this life of true idealism from his early teens. What should his attitude be towards other people? I should of course cover many things here, but I would like to dwell on one point in particular. His attitude towards others should largely be one of *surprise*. He should be surprised, truly astonished, at the lack of ideals he sees in so many people around him or at the false ideals they at times pursue.

Surprise

He should be surprised. I think it is worth examining this reaction, this *attitude* of surprise. Because it is a factor of the highest importance both for the good defence of his own Christian ideals and for their communication to others.

A sign of the weakness of the faith and ideals of many Christian today is the fact that they show little or no surprise at current events, ideas or attitudes that are not only unchristian but are not even human. Clearly, this lack of psychological reaction, this absence of an intimate and indignant rejection of the errors or aberrations in question, weakens not only their own defence against such evils, but also their very capacity to convince other persons that such things in fact are evil.

One of the first bits of advice I got about teaching comes to my mind. I was told that a teacher's simple *look* of surprise sometimes obtains a more rapid change of conduct in a child than would a reasoned explanation. Put on a look, I was told, of "How is it possible a ten-year-old boy can do a thing like

120

that?". . . and you'll see the results. I liked the idea. But the results were far below expectation, and have taught me to distrust the formula, at least with children of that precise age. My experience is that, no matter how surprised you look, the boy can look back at you, as cool as a cucumber, as if to say, "I wonder just when you will learn that a ten-year-old boy is capable of doing a thing like that and much more besides. . . ." His teacher's face of surprise leaves him absolutely cold. He probably even finds it funny.

However, I think it wasn't the teaching technique but the age that was mistaken. The surprised-look reaction, which bounces off the ten- or eleven-year-old, can in fact be quite effective with an older person, and especially with adolescents who, between the ages of fourteen and twenty, are tremendously sensitive to what others think of them and are very scared of making fools of themselves.

Who is making a fool of himself?

Moreover, applying this specifically to what we are talking about—the apostolate—it is not a question of a stratagem or an affected reaction. The reaction should be real. It is simply a question of not failing to be surprised at attitudes that are in fact surprising.

Here we have to make up for lost ground, for in some inexplicable way we have let a good deal of the psychological advantage pass to the opposite side. So much so that many people today are "surprised" if it turns out that one *does* go to Mass, or has *not* read the latest best-selling obscenity, or has *not* seen the latest pornographic film.

Given this situation, it seems urgent to me not only to re-stress the sense of sin in these matters, but also to recover the sense of the ridiculous. Otherwise some people are going to keep on thinking, "Of course I know that if I see or read this, I'll be committing a sin, but if I don't see it, I'll be making a fool of myself", whereas the truth is that, if they do see it, they are not only committing a sin but they are also in fact making fools of themselves! Of course it is more important to convince them that they are committing a sin, but, to begin with, it may be easier to get them realize they are making fools of

121

themselves. For they are. And we should be surprised at it; and show our surprise.

There are, then, two points to be emphasized here. Our surprise may be the best defence against the possible weakening of our own firmness in principles and conduct. After all, if a person does not react with amazement at the absurdity—at the intellectual poverty and the human degradation—of the postures held by some Christians, he may eventually come to regard them as reasonable or respectable. . . . But our surprise may also prove to be a healthy shock for these inconsistent Christians. It may be a new experience for them, and one needed precisely in order to give a jolt to their dulled minds. If the jolt sets their minds working, they may begin to realize the extraordinary degree to which they are being fooled or are fooling themselves.

It is surprising, really surprising, if a person states that he does not believe in God, or if he maintains, as a reasonable proposition, the idea that the world emerged, unaided, from nothing. It is surprising if he states this. But it would be even more surprising if we were to treat his statement as if it were a reasonable and intelligent position, and began to argue seriously about it. It is not a serious position. It is absurd. Our first natural reaction, therefore, should be to laugh at it. After that (also out of charity), we should try to get him to look at the matter in a more mature fashion. In a word, we should try to get him to *think*.

It is surprising if a person who says he is a Catholic does not pray or go to Mass on Sundays; or goes, but obviously under the impression that he is fulfilling a senseless obligation, and without the least awareness that he is receiving a divine gift. It is absurd.

It is surprising if a person proclaims himself to be more "liberated" because he rejects the need for any type of self-control in sexual matters. It is absurd because he is clearly enslaving himself.

It is surprising if a person 'justifies' his attendance at a notoriously pornographic show by appealing to what certain critics have said about its "artistic" value. To put on airs about the *culture* or refinement which he has drawn from a show of that nature is simply pathetic and absurd.

It is surprising when someone defends abortion in the name of *humanity* or when he suggests that it all boils down to the "right" to a woman has over her *own* body. . . . It is absurd.

It is surprising if a communist puts himself forward as a defender of freedom or democracy. One has only to think of the "democratic freedoms" lived in Russia, in order to classify him, if not as a hypocrite, at least as a comedian. It is absurd.

Any Christian with an average formation can easily see what is sinful or mistaken in the examples given, or in other examples along the same lines. But many fail to realize how poverty-stricken they are, how hollow, how ridiculous and how absurd. The Christian who is really in contact with Christ, as his ideal and as his Friend, will scarcely fail to realize it. And his reaction will be one of amazement. And his amazement will startle many people out of their sleep.

I've seen so many cases. The boy whose friend tells him that he hardly practices his religion, and who reacts: "But, is it possible that you don't go to Mass?". . . "What, you just don't care about receiving Holy Communion?". . ."But, do you seriously mean you haven't been to Confession for six months?". . . And the look of surprise—which is not put on, which is genuine—shakes him. Because normally these companions have some faith left, however drugged it may be. And what can rouse and waken them, at least to begin with, is not so much reasoned argument but a friend's amazement: "But, are you mad?". . . And they may well begin to think, "Perhaps he's right. Perhaps I am mad."

"Have you really gone to see that film? You're nuts. . . . Don't you realize that if you go on like that, your life is going to fall to pieces? You're going to become a slave to obsession, don't you see that? And have you thought that you won't have the slightest chance of a happy marriage later on because no decent girl will accept you?". . . Each of these questions can be a hammer-blow awakening them, because they know in their hearts that all of it is true.

And if it's the case of the comfort-loving egoist: "So, you see no need to serve other people? You are quite happy just looking after yourself? What a miserable life!"

And if it is a Marxist: "I agree with you that we should try to build a more just society. But we won't achieve it by spreading violence and hatred. . . Besides, are you really satisfied to be a pawn of the State, a lump of matter, no more, in a world where no one has any real worth because no one has any personal destiny? Does such a poor ideal really satisfy you? How pitiful! How absurd!"

Saving idealism from bankruptcy

Before ending let us recall those words of Msgr Escrivá that I quoted at the beginning. "Young people have always had a great capacity for enthusiasm, for big things, for high ideals, for everything that is genuine." *For everything that is genuine!* Christ is genuine, even though we Christians often are not. Christianity is a genuine ideal, an ideal that fills to over-flowing the noblest desires of the human heart. And its genuine nature is bound to stand out more clearly, in all its colossal attractiveness, precisely in a world like ours which is so filled with false "ideals"—whose falseness is each day becoming harder for people not to see.

Perhaps in former times, many men did not reach the full truth (the Truth of Christ), or did not accept the true Ideal—which is Christ—because they stopped half-way. They never managed to get beyond partial and exclusively human ideals. And there they remained, in a posture that combined a certain ease (since partial ideals do not generally ask for too great a commitment in too many areas at the same time) with a certain sincerity, because their minds were captivated by that part of the truth they found in those ideals and which , if one did not look too deeply into the matter, seemed to give the stamp of an all-embracing and genuine ideal. And in this way many men—sincere men, no doubt, though not very deep men—were idealists. Idealists and enthusiasts of ideals of equality, of liberty, of fraternity, of the independence of their country, of the emancipation of slaves, etc.

These ideals were genuine—as far as they went. And their partial authenticity was often enough to capture the hearts of the young. But today authenticity seems everywhere to be on the verge of bankruptcy. The noble names and terms of the great human ideals of the past are bandied about, as much as or more than ever before. But they are being given a content and meaning that is so low, so degraded, even at times so anti-human, that it no longer seems possible for anyone to be taken in, unless he wants to.

When the "ideals" offered to men are: in the name of love, sex: in the name of freedom, licence and selfishness; in the name of the right to a full development of one's own personality, contempt for the standards and rights of others; in the name of independence and personal maturity, the rejection of any type of authority and the consequent incapacity for service; in the name of responsibility or democratic participation, idle and sterile protest; in the name of political or social justice, violence and hatred. . . . When this is what we are offered, what, one may ask, is lacking to have human idealism declared utterly bankrupt?

It is not we Christians, however, who will declare it bankrupt. We can save it. If young people (and in some way, all men in their hearts) are looking for genuine ideals, the moment could hardly be more favorable. All the partial human ideals have failed or been emptied of their content. All that is needed now is to expose the falseness or hypocrisy of the libertine, materialist or marxist "ideals". This is the task now facing us Christians. It will be easily done if we have more faith, more daring, and a keener sense of the ridiculous. Then an entire world of young people and older people will have no alternative (nor will they, I feel, want any alternative) but to turn to the only truly genuine ideal, the only full ideal that is neither false nor insufficient, the only ideal capable of appealing to all men, of enthusing and filling them, of uniting and purifying and elevating them: the ideal which is Christ.

8

The family and the permissive society

The permissive society turns violent

Lots of us have the impression that the modern world is succumbing to violence. In the face of so many acts of sheer brutality and terrorism, no doubt we often ask ourselves: how can some people be so irresponsible, unprincipled and violent?

The answer, I would suggest, lies partly in ourselves. We are all partly to blame for the growing violence of the world we live in, because we tolerate—or perhaps even seek and approve—a permissive society. The logic is simple. A permissive society means a society which professes no fixed moral principles. Such a society inevitably generates a large mass of irresponsible people. And when people in general are irresponsible, a growing percentage are going to turn out violent.

The one restraining principle, in a permissive society, is that conduct should not be anti-social. But, saving this, nothing else is really wrong, anything can be right; it all depends on the feelings and choices of each individual. And when young people grow up in a society where they have been taught that there are no absolute and objective moral values, but everything is relative and subjective, they are not likely to put what they are told are collectivist interests above their personal desires or whims. When the mass of young people have been taught that nothing is to be held sacred, that nothing merits absolute respect, it is only logical that many of them end up in fact respecting *nothing* at all—nothing personal, nothing social: not property, nor law, nor liberty, nor life. Little more is needed to make them criminals or terrorists. And if some go that way, it is the very society they despise, rob and terrorise that has helped turn them into terrorists.

A permissive society creates a climate that fosters violence. . . . But is this a thesis that can be proved? I think so. After all, permissiveness centres mainly on the question of sex. And it should be obvious to anyone with an iota of common sense that sex is an area of human conduct filled with potential for violence. To deny this would leave one unable to account for the phenomenon of rape and other whole chapters of criminal history.

Contrary to what is suggested by much modern propaganda, sex and love are not the same. Subordinated to love and to its evident procreative function, sex is a noble and God-given reality that finds its proper expression in married love. But sex is man's most unruly and explosive instinct. It does not easily let itself be subordinated to anything. Once the sexual impulse is aroused, it wants immediate satisfaction, and it wants it on its own terms, as an end in itself.

The paradoxes of man are many. And they are specially intense in the sphere of sex. Sex which can, with an effort, be integrated into man's most noble power of love, can also—if no effort is made—be one of the most brutal and violent expressions of his selfishness.[1] Uncontrolled sex tends to run wild. It is destructive. The first thing it destroys, in its self-seeking, is love, for love and selfishness are mutual enemies. And it can destroy many other things besides.

Abortionism leads to terrorism

Our permissive societies not only tell people that there is little or no need to control the violence of their sexual impulses, but tend to surround them with constant sexual stimulation. The inevitable result is growing violence.

The philosophers of permissiveness do not like this talk of there being a violent element in sex, though they are scarcely so naive as to deny it. If pushed they would probably say that, though not against violence in sex, they are against sex that *does* violence *to others*, i.e. against their will. A permissive society would therefore regard rape, for instance, as wrong. But its philosophers would maintain that all other forms of sexual conduct should be considered morally, socially and legally acceptable; not only whatever an individual chooses to do sexually, in the sphere of his own private thoughts and actions, but also what two or more people—married or single, of the same or opposite sex—*consent* to do together.

127

But a good look at permissiveness will tell us that, however much consent there may be, violence is always done to someone by permissive sex. In the long list of permissive "achievements" in the field of sex or sex-related conduct, it is very arguably true that quite a lot of *moral* violence is frequently done in the case of extra-marital affairs (violence done to one spouse's right to expect loyalty from the other), and much more so in that of divorce (violence very often done again to one of the spouses; and certainly to the children). Do the children normally consent to the divorce? Is tremendous violence not done to their desire that their mother and father should live and learn to get on together? And it is unanswerably true that the most extreme physical violence—the killing of an innocent child—is the essence of abortion. To legalise abortion is to legalise violence. A society that does not fight against abortionists has therefore very soon to fight against terrorists. But it will be a losing battle. For terrorism cannot really be combated with police force. It can only be combated by educating people in moral principles, above all in the fundamental social principle of respect for life.

Violence and pornography

In any case, leaving aside these questions of the violence *to others* that a permissive society condones, it is also clear that the person who gives free rein, in any circumstance, to his every sexual desire, does violence *to himself*, permits violence within himself. And this is the essential reason why a permissive society leads to all sorts of violence. Once people are led to believe—as permissiveness teaches them—that it is perfectly alright to stimulate within oneself, and seek to satisfy, the violent impulses of sex, then it becomes progressively harder, and eventually impossible, to teach or convince them that it is wrong for them to follow other violent impulses: hatred, the desire to rob or kill or seek revenge. . . . It is useless to tell a person to respect society or to respect others, if at the same time you are telling him that he need not respect or restrain himself.

In any case, it is not only a matter of common sense that pornography leads to violence. It is also by now a well-documented fact. One would do well to read Chapter Three of the Longford Report on Pornography. The chapter, entitled "Violence and Pornography" points out how pornography tends more and more to present the violent—sadistic or masochistic—aspect of sex itself; how it has been consciously used as a means to foster political violence (as in Hitler's Germany) or social instability (modern marxist tactics in Western countries); and how "hard core" pornography fosters hatred, aggression and alienation and is clearly a main cause of the growing criminality and violence of our Western societies.

Return to censorship? . . .

The situation is surely crying out for some form of control. In fact—though this obliges me to use one of the dirtiest words in our language—I would say that it is crying out for some form of *censorship*! . . .

"Censorship?", I can hear some reader cry out incredulously. "But is it possible that anyone nowadays can defend the idea of censorship seriously?" Very seriously. But the censorship I am thinking of is probably not the type the incredulous reader has in mind. It is essentially the *self-censorship* we referred to earlier (pp.90f). The whole matter merits some further remarks.

Yes, I know that modern man says that he prizes freedom as one of his highest goods; that he regards censorship as one of the greatest traditional enemies of freedom. I know too that it is commonly believed—or at least affirmed—that the progressive abolition of censorship has enabled millions to enjoy a new freedom of which they were formerly deprived.

Let me then assure the reader that I, for one, have no desire to deprive the mass of people of their freedom; just the contrary. But I do suggest that, though what we want today is more freedom, it is not what we are getting. What we are getting is sexual anarchy, and what we are being submitted to is sexual exploitation and slavery. Nothing could be farther removed from freedom.

Freedom and exploitation

"Freedom for all" sounds a noble maxim. But history has shown that freedom for all generally means more and more freedom for the strong, the rich, the clever or the unscrupulous, and less and less freedom for the rest of mankind. It means freedom for the few and some form of serfdom for the many.

Absolute freedom in the commercial or industrial spheres was vehemently preached one hundred and fifty years ago. But practically no one defends it nowadays. The history of nineteenth century liberalism in these fields shows that a few men, if unrestrained by some form of government controls, tend to exploit the masses.

Why then should we be surprised to find something similar happening when the liberal principle of unrestricted freedom is applied to the sexual sphere? Surely only the very naive could deny that one of the first results of the abolition of censorship has been to turn pornography into big business, and to make multi-millionaires out of the pornographic businessmen? Nor is it hard to see why pornography, as business, is specially big and specially profitable, and why, therefore, immensely rich interest are involved in maintaining the anti-censorship prejudice among the public, and sustaining the fiction of freedom which enables the market to prosper.

If one can stimulate and then exploit an *artificial* appetite like the taste for tobacco, it should obviously be much easier to exploit—through stimulation—a *natural* and very strong appetite like the sex appetite. Young people have a potential sales resistance in regard to cigarettes. They generally don't enjoy their first experience of smoking. Therefore, the tobacco manufacturer has to stir other motives. And so, by direct advertising, he creates a social atmosphere in which to smoke gives a he-man image, is mod, or "with it". The pornographer has a potentially easier public, in one sense. Pornography is attractive to man's animal instinct. But at the same time it is repellent to his religious instinct, to his human conscience and—especially in the case of girls and women—to the sense of modesty. These forces which make for sales resistance have, therefore, to be overcome. And this is done by creating a social climate where sexual licence is called freedom, and sexual restraint is condemned as old-fashioned, Victorian, unnatural, inhibiting, etc. The advertising here is indirect. But it is a veritable barrage. And the pornographers'

130

advertisers— perhaps unwitting, perhaps unpaid—abound among philosophers, psychologist, artists, script-writers, politicians. . . .

The slave market

Another point is that the seller's ideal, in any business, is the regular customer, the habituated consumer. The tobacco market is so sure and so profitable, because it is made up of *captive* buyers. The same applies to drink. When the market is drugs or sex, one can even speak of *enslaved* buyers. The exploitation of slaves—especially when people pay to be slaves—is an infallible way to make an unscrupulous fortune. And all in the name of liberty! The exploitation is all the more obvious when one recalls that commercialised sex is for buyers who are "dupes". It is a fraud. It fascinates; it promises much; it gives little—a satisfaction that leaves the consumer dissatisfied, and so wanting more.

In the liberal industrial society of the last century, the common men had little power to resist the exploitation of their lives, even if they wished to. They either worked or starved. Millions today are objects of an exploitation which does not (at least normally) reduce them to living in slums and hovels, which consists not in their material oppression but in their spiritual and human degradation. It is an infinitely worse exploitation. Nevertheless, compared with the last century, it is evident that men in today's liberal permissive society can resist being exploited, if they wish. The trouble is that many apparently do not wish. . . .

At the beginning of laissez-faire capitalism government policy was one of non-intervention. Under an awakening public conscience and growing public pressure, governments were gradually obliged to live up to their responsibilities to intervene and prevent the exploitation of the weak. There seems to be little public sensitivity today about sexual exploitation and sexual degradation, and there is therefore little public pressure on governments to prevent them. It is evident that, until the public wakes up, nothing effective will be done to remedy the situation.

Maturity and corruptibility

This whole subject is one of the fastest growing areas of lying and insincerity in our modern world. Are we adults all that different from young people? Are we seriously suggesting that what can corrupt a youth aged sixteen cannot possibly corrupt an adult aged twenty-six or fifty-six? As if the eighteen or twenty-one watershed, which gives a certain presumption of maturity can warrant an equal presumption of incorruptibility!

Few people profess to be unconcerned about the pornography problem. It is too big and obvious for that. Yet, time and again, in one country after another, investigation committees and work parties come up with proposals which, if one hesitates to brand them as insincere, can only be described as incredibly superficial, The proposals, in a nut-shell, come down to this: "Censorship, for young people? *Of course*! Censorship, for grown-ups? *Absolutely not!*"

On the one hand, there are pressing appeals for effective measures to permit our young people to live in an atmosphere free from the corruption caused by pornography. On the other hand, there are the most indignant rejections of any measure designed to cleanse from the same corruption the atmosphere in which adults move.

There is agreement, on the one hand, that pornography is a threat to the freedom of young people, and a danger to their normal psychic and emotional development. There is equal agreement on the other, the censorship is a threat to the freedom of adults, and an insult to their maturity.

It seems incredible that anyone can seriously maintain this double posture. One is immediately struck, to begin with, by the practical impossibility of building up any useful result from such contradictory foundations. The "freedoms" which grown-ups claim for themselves must necessarily make the controls for young people ineffective. After all, young people and grown-ups do not move in two totally different worlds nor are their "atmospheres" so easily separated in practice. But what is much harder to understand is the concept of man or society on which the proposals are presumably based.

If they are based on anything, it would seem to be on one or other of two suppositions

132

a) that at a certain age or level of maturity, one is no longer in danger of being affected or corrupted by pornography; or

b) that at a certain age, it is no one else's business if one wishes to corrupt oneself. Let us consider each of these suppositions.

Intelligent? sincere? normal?

It seems possible to adopt the first attitude—that immunisation from pornography comes with the years—only as a result of having switched off one's mind. In such cases, therefore, the only remedy likely to be effective is some form of shock therapy, to get people to *think*. Since one of the principles often enunciated (though not always practised) in the permissive society is that it is presumptuous to judge others, my "therapy", in dealing with the cases we are considering, is not to judge, but to try to get each one to judge himself or herself. I should add that occasions have not been lacking to practise the therapy with young people no less than with grown-ups. This also, unfortunately, is logical enough. When adults act and speak as if their "maturity" had somehow immunised them form any degrading effects of pornography, young people (who, for good or bad, tend to imitate their elders) quickly take up the same line, and are only too anxious to affirm that they too are mature and equally immunised. But let us take a specific case and the application of the therapy.

A fifteen or seventeen year-old boy or girl comes to me and says, "I have read or seen such-and-such" (some novel or film well known to be pornographic), "and really I didn't find anything so special or disturbing in it. It didn't affect me . . . ." My stock way of answering this pseudo-maturity is more or less as follows.

"Well, of course I can't judge you. You have to judge yourself. But what I *can* say is that anyone who has seen that film or read that book and says he hasn't been affected by it, cannot be three things at the same time. He can't be intelligent, sincere and normal, all at once. He can be two of these things, or possess two of these qualities, but not the three together." And I explain: "If you, who say you have been left unmoved by this work, are normal and sincere; i.e. if you are a normally constituted person as far as sex goes, and at the same time you really think you are telling me the truth, then you are not intelligent, you are not deep, you don't really know yourself. For this work affects all normal people. Therefore it has affected you, without your realising it . . . ."

"Of course this may not be the case. There is a second possibility: that you are normal and intelligent; i.e. you have normal sexual reactions and you know yourself. but in that case, you are not being sincere. Of course that work has affected you, and you know it. But you are not telling me the truth. . . ."

"But that, again, is a possibility you must judge. Far be it from me to make any judgment. You know yourself. Because, after all, there is a third possibility: that you are sincere and intelligent; i.e. that you indeed know yourself and are indeed telling me the truth; in other words, that that work has really not affected you. . . . But then, you are. . . . Well, I leave the conclusion up to you . . . ."

I've had more than one indignant reaction; "Hey, I'm not that." To which I reply: "I didn't say you were. I'm only pointing out alternatives. It's you who have to apply them."

Pseudo-maturity

But are these alternatives valid only for teenagers? Are adults too not capable of a *pseudo-maturity*? How switched off has the brain got to get before one suggests that a person can be corrupted at sixteen and not at thirty six? If a person is in fact corrupted at sixteen, he will presumably grow into a corrupt adult. And then the problem will be to un-corrupt him. Or are there no corrupt—or corruptible—adults?

The alternatives—sincere, intelligent, normal—which apply at sixteen apply equally at thirty six or at fifty. If therefore one meets whole masses of people nowadays who claim to be so mature that pornography no longer affects them, what is one to think? One certainly hesitates to conclude that there can possibly be so many queers around. But then one is driven to the conclusion that many "mature" people today are either dreadfully unthinking or else unthinkingly insincere. My

134

own feeling is that they are probably a mixture of both; that is why I would like to say that the lines that follow, though they may hit hard, are not meant to be negative. For they are written in an attempt to jerk unthinking people into thought, and in the conviction that if they really do begin to think they will discover the insincerity of their own position; and begin to be sincere.

Turning sin into virtue

Our modern adult world, which prides itself on being "liberated" and thanks God (or perhaps just itself) on not being like all former generations of mankind, is guilty not only of Pharisaism much more repellent that that of the Pharisee of the Gospel[2], but also of hypocrisy much worse than the Victorian hypocrisy it professes particularly to despise. The Victorians—so at least we are told—did wrong, and pretended they did not do it. Our modern permissivist does wrong, and says it is right. The Victorian sinned and, hiding it, wished himself to be regarded as virtuous. The modern permissivist sins and, proclaiming his sin, wishes it to be regarded as virtue. The Victorian at least knew what sin was, though—perhaps—he did little to avoid it. The modern permissivist proclaims there is no such thing as sin, and so he has nothing to avoid or repent of. He presents himself as sinless. He is the self-proclaimed saint.

If there is such a generation gap today, if young people often have little respect for their elders, it is largely because the younger generation senses the hypocrisy, or at least the falseness, of this all too common adult attitude towards the question of censorship: "Censorship for young people; of course. Censorship for us? Absurd! They are young; we must not let them be corrupted. We are mature, and incorruptible." Small wonder that young people have little more than contempt for the defenders of such a double standard of morality.

The right to corrupt oneself?

As we suggested earlier, the double standard may be based on a slightly different supposition: not that adults are incorruptible, but that if they want to corrupt themselves, that is their personal business, and no one else—no private individual and no public authority—has a right to interfere.

This at least is not a moralising position. Its exponents have no interest in morality. Their one slogan is "freedom". "We want freedom. We claim freedom: freedom to do what we like. Now that we have it, let no one try to take it from us".

Two comments could be made about this position. One is about the use of the word freedom. I do not think these people should be let get away with claiming they have found a new freedom. They have not. They have found an old slavery. A sex-addict is no more free than is a drug-addict or an alcoholic. If he chooses to go the way of addiction, that is his business. But let him not say it is the way of freedom. A man is free not when he is not ruled by external laws, but when the rules himself; when he is master of himself. And these people do not rule themselves. They are ruled by their passions. And the slavery that comes from within is worse than any slavery imposed from outside.[3]

The second comment is to question the supposed "right" a person has to corrupt himself if he wants to. A person will certainly do it, if he wants to; just as a person will rob or murder—or commit suicide—if he wants to. But does he have a *right* to do these things? Most certainly not. We have the rights which God has given us, no more. We have the *power* to contravene his will. But we have not the right to do so.[4]

Besides, rights cannot exist without duties. A person's right to life means that everyone else has a duty to respect his life. And he, theirs. I have the right that my neighbour respects my property and my person. But I also have the right that he respects *himself*. No one has a right to defile the street. No one has the right to degrade the world. No one has the right to degrade himself. We are not disconnected pieces, in a disconnected world. What each of us does or is or lets himself become has an effect—for good or bad—on those around him. That is why to degrade oneself is in some way to offend the rest of humanity, just as it is, more importantly, to offend God.

Turning people into objects

Sex is a divine gift, a sacred function by which human love is, in marriage, given a unique expression of union that associates it with God's creativity. Pornography involves an essential degradation of this sacred reality of sex. For pornography tends to arouse sex for sex's sake, and not sex for the sake of love and procreation. And that is to degrade its meaning and function, reducing it to the level of animal instinct whose one purpose is to seek immediate sensual satisfaction. And when people give free rein to their animal instincts, they become in fact more and more like animals, and less and less able to respect one another as persons.

On an even broader plane than the one we are at present considering, it is true that a person not in control of his appetites or instincts cannot relate to others in a truly human fashion, for his uncontrolled impulses prevent him from respecting them. He will use or abuse others as objects; he will not respect them as persons. The capitalist, dominated by greed, will exploit his workers, though he will no doubt rationalise his conduct. The terrorist, dominated by exalted nationalism, by blind hatred or by a desire for revenge, will kidnap, torture or murder innocent victims. The pornographer or, more specifically, the pornographer's client—the person dominated and obsessed by sex—will equally exploit others if he can; for other people interest him only insofar as they can serve his obsessive appetite. In others he doesn't see persons, he too sees only objects—to be desired, to be used, to be abused, to be discarded. Respect for others becomes meaninless to his befogged mind and impossible to his weakened will and ever more selfish nature.

The permissive woman

The permissive society makes for selfish people, and selfish people tend not to trust one another. One of the sad though not surprising characteristics of our permissive societies is the growing atmosphere of mistrust, especially between the sexes. Men and women, boys and girls, tend to trust each other less and less. It is logical; degraded people do not trust one another.

The permissive man degrades himself through indulging his sensuality. The permissive woman may do likewise. More often her motive is simply vanity; or else greed. In any case it is equally selfish, and no less degrading.

Greed is assuredly the main motive of some women who let themselves be paraded as sex objects, for presumably they require to be paid—perhaps substantially—to let themselves be photographed for a particular type of magazine, or take part in certain films or shows. More curious, also because more frequent, is the case of other women—women, more-over, who probably regard themselves as "respectable"—who actually *pay* (and at times substantially) to *parade themselves* as sex objects. It is simple feminine vanity that moves them, no more. But at times feminine vanity is just as bad, just as selfish and just as degrading, as masculine sensuality. The vanity of many women today has so enslaved them to fashion that, by the clothes they wear or their way of behaving, they seem to be inviting men—they almost seem bent on obliging them—to treat them as objects. Their vanity, just as much as the pin-up's cupidity, seeks to exact its payment from men's sensuality.

While on this subject one could well add a word on modesty—that apparently forgotten or despised feminine virtue of yesteryear. Modesty—in a woman's way of dressing or acting—is simply an expression of her *determination to be treated as a person* by men; and her refusal to be dragged down to the level of an object.

Children and their parents' loyalty

I realise of course that some people today will not listen to these arguments. The reason is simple: they will not listen to their own conscience. A person's conscience—if he is prepared to listen to it—tells him clearly enough when he is degrading himself or degrading others.

Some people, therefore, are indifferent to all arguments. I am not really writing for them. I would rather now write particularly for parents, for I am sure that, whatever their formation, they are not indifferent to one thing, namely their own children. And yet there is a grave danger today that, if they do not stop to think and take a sincere look at things, some parents may be guilty of betraying the very children they love.

Parents who allow themselves permissive liberties are in fact guilty of such a betrayal. I am not referring just to the obvious and extreme betrayal of the father or mother who has an affair with someone else or who gets a divorce. I am thinking of the much more frequent betrayal of the parents who simply practise the double morality we have referred to earlier. "You children cannot see or read this; we can."

As pointed out earlier,[5] children have a *right* to their parents' loyalty; in this matter they have a right to their parents' sincerity, self-restraint and example. The father or mother who reads or attends a pornographic work not only offends God and degrades himself or herself, but violates their children's right to have parents they can look up to.

This reinforces the conclusion of an earlier chapter: the need for *self-censorship*. The practical moral point here is that each one needs to be *his own censor*: to have the clarity of mind to realise what works can deform or degrade him, and the sincerity and strength of will to avoid them.

If parents see that the public authorities are doing little to combat the moral contamination of the atmosphere their children have to breathe and grow in, then it is up to them—the parents—to do more. They cannot be afraid to exercise authority with their children and to make demands of them. But these demands have little chance of being listened to (and none whatsoever of being respected) if the parents are not making at least equally strong demands on themselves. Let us be sincere. If parents really love their children, and want therefore to protect them from the pernicious effects of pornography, the only effective (and the only honest) argument is: "To see or read such a show or work would mean offending God and degrading oneself. Therefore we cannot let you see it, just as we cannot—*and will not*—let ourselves see or read it either."

What am I prepared to eat?

Self-censorship is simply one expression of self-control, and self-control is essential for individual and social freedom.[6] No one would suggest that self-control is always easy. But it is made a lot easier if one switches on one's mind and exercises a bit of common sense.

Let us suppose I go to a supermarket with the intention of buying food and something to drink. Let us suppose too that there is a series of foodstuffs and beverages on offer, which look very appetising and smell very nice, but which I have good reason to know contain poison . . . . What do I do?—I buy something else! Thank God there are plenty of other things to choose from that also taste quite good, and are in fact wholesome.

And if the situation developed where most of the food-stuffs on display were poisoned? I'd still not buy them. It would mean having to shop round a bit more, but in the end I'm sure I'd find some edible food. And if the moment were to come when practically everything seemed nice-looking but poisoned?. . . Well, I guess I'd just have to grow my own food! And perhaps look around for a few other sensible citizens ready to join in a wholesome-food-producing cooperative.

What if some (or many) of my fellow citizens didn't seem to believe that the food was poisoned, and ate it? What if they didn't seem to take notice of the subsequent symptoms of food-poisoning (though the symptoms could in fact be easily seen by anyone taking a proper look)? . . . I still would not eat . . . . And if they told me not to be old-fashioned, if they taunted me with being hidebound by Victorian prejudices, if they insisted that my reluctance to eat betrayed a lack of maturity, or a non-liberated personality?. . . I still don't think I'd let myself be moved. I trust that my fear of suicide would prove stronger than my fear of public opinion, especially of such a stupid public opinion. What if the insistence came from friendlier quarter: "Come on, old chap. Don't be such a stick-in-the-mud. Enjoy the fun. It's great stuff, and it tastes so good?" I'd probably answer: "I don't question its attraction. I don't even question its taste (though I do wonder about the *after*-taste . . .). I simply say it is poison" (and remember the most dangerous poisons are those that look good and taste good).

What if a particular friend urged me to share in the goodies he had purchased and was consuming? Frankly, if I saw a friend (or anyone I cared for, however slightly) drinking a poisoned Coca-cola, or a scotch-on-the-rocks laced with arsenic, and couldn't manage to persuade him it was poisoned, not only would I refuse to partake, but . . . well, I'm inclined to think that, reasoned argument having failed, what I would do in all friendship is to knock the glass out of his hand and break it. And if he protested: "What the so-and-so do you think you are doing? That was *my* drink!", I'd reply; "I've done you a *favour*. You were poisoning yourself." And if I did not act so—out of *respect for other people's freedom*—I think I'd be a very poor friend. God preserve us from liberal friends whose principles make them stand by indifferently while they watch us commit unwitting suicide.

Pornography and poison

One scarcely needs to spell out the application of the parable. Shakespeare did not actually say that "all the world's a supermarket", though he might well be tempted to do so if he were alive today. And he would probably be capable of adding a few choice comments on seeing that whole sections of the supermarket are being filled with pornography: theatre, novels, films, television, entertainment in general, advertising. . . .

What is one to do when offered such tempting goods of such doubtful quality? What is one to do? *Think*. Is thinking all that hard?

I am offered pornography. So what? Even if my super-natural sense did not tell me that to buy, read, see or advertise it is an offence against God which destroys the divine life of grace in my soul, my common sense should tell me that it is poison to my natural life, that it threatens to murder all my human possibilities of happiness: obsessing me, depriving me of the freedom to love, making it more and more impossible for me to relate with respect to any person of the opposite sex or, if that is my calling, to find a noble and tender and lasting love in marriage.

Since pornography is poison, I avoid it. If this means having to avoid certain shows, programmes, novels or maga-zines, so what? There are still plenty of other unpolluted works around which I can enjoy. And if someone were to tell me not to be a Victorian, I'd tell him or her not to be a fool. *I* do not consider myself a Victorian, just a normal person with an ounce of common sense. But in any case, it is better to be a live Victorian than a dead fool.

And if someone shows me a pornographic magazine, I tear it up. "What the blazes have you done? That was my magazine!"—"That was your poison. I've done you a favour. If you are bent on committing suicide, please go and do it privately and don't try to involve others." It's a peculiar rule of life; but, whether or not the number of the foolish is limitless, some people do in fact seem to believe that foolishness is made less if we can all be fools together: that poison won't prove quite so lethal if we can get everyone to take it. They seem to forget that history has seen whole cities destroyed by plague, because no one woke up to the fact that it was a plague until it was too late. More people are being destroyed by the pornographic plague today than were ever killed by the bubonic.

The half poisoned cake

To say, "No, I refuse to see it or read it", when one knows or suspects that the work in question is offensive to God and degrading to man: that is self-control, that is self-censorship. To get up and walk openly out of a show when, contrary to one's expectations, it turns out to be degrading: that is self-control and self-censorship.

Perhaps we could add a word about the work that one has reason to believe is a first-class production in other respects (plot, acting, camera work, etc.), but has its sprinkling of pornographic scenes, the quite unnecessary poisoned icing-sugar on top, or inside. What to do?

Let us go back to the supermarket, because our food-shopping can once more help us solve the case. There before me on the counter is an absolutely fabulously looking cake; and perhaps the management is even inviting me to try it, to see how good it tastes. But it is the same story: I am morally certain it is poisoned, at least in parts. *Ergo*? I do not eat! No; not even if it were gratis! I don't see any compensation in being poisoned free of charge . . . (though I do see that what is utterly absurd is to *pay* to be poisoned, however much this may in fact be what so many people do today).

Now things could be different if the poisoned portions were quite localised and if someone (someone I could trust) assured me that they had all been cut out of the cake, and that what was left was in fact perfectly good eating, absolutely uncontaminated gourmet's delight. . . . In such a case, presented with a thoroughly expurgated cake, I would probably have no hesitation in eating it. The only question is: who is going to do the expurgating for me? I myself? Frankly, I'm not sure that I trust myself. After all, one would have to detect in some way the exact location of the poisoned sections. This obviously requires a palate sensitive to poison (to *nice*-tasting poison). It especially requires an ability to spot when one is passing from harmless eating to poisoned eating, and this, I suppose, must inevitably involve chewing some slight distance into the poisoned sections. That's the moment when I think a I'm capable of fooling myself, and with a "Oh, it can't be that bad, and it does taste good . . .", carrying on and swallowing the whole piece; and so having to pay the whole price afterwards.

Nothing to lose?

The fact is, I repeat, that I'm not sure how far I can trust myself. Cleaning up a poisoned cake really requires a very sensitive palate, in order to know where to stop, coupled with a very strong will, in order to be able to do so; or else—perhaps—it simply requires a total immunity to poison. I certainly don't have this latter immunity. And though I think I have the required sensitivity of palate, I cannot guarantee the strength of my will. So, all told, if there has to be cake-expurgation, I'd prefer to have the expurgating done by someone else. (Though I will add, as a general and rather annoyed reflection, that I cannot help feeling that life would be a lot simpler if the cake-producers would be more careful about the extraordinary amount of poison that seems of late to be creeping into their cake-mixtures).

This is the way I feel about those best-selling films or novels, with their pornographic plums and sugar-icing, those unnecessary scenes thrown in, from the producer's pure bounty, as "free" extras. If I can't find someone else to do (or, really, to undo) the dirty work for me (Oh shades of that old and elephant-hided benefactor, the public censor!), I'm afraid I'll just eat elsewhere.

I'm sorry, friends. But if mistrusting oneself or being afraid of unnecessary danger is a sign of immaturity and unliberatedness, well, put me down as decidedly immature and hopelessly unliberated. My only consolation will have to be that here at least I am, still alive.

James Baldwin, the American writer, speaks somewhere of the danger to society of the presence, in it, of people who "have nothing to lose". I feel I have everything to lose; or, with God's help, everything to gain. But in order not to lose one's freedom, or one's soul, it is essential to realise that one *can* lose it, and to be able to recognise and avoid those things capable of depriving one of it. In 1965, during the twenty fifth Anniversary of the Battle of Britain, someone asked Ginger Lacy, the RAF's No. 1 Ace of the 1940 dog-fights, how had he survived, and what qualities a fighter pilot needs to survive. His answer was crisp and clear: "I survived because I was just bloody lucky. Luck is the main quality a fighter pilot has to have. You must also be able to get good and healthily scared, otherwise you just get yourself killed. I knew some fellows who weren't frightened, and they have been dead for twenty five years."

Self-censorship is just part of self-control. And self-control and self-vigilance are essential if one wants to survive. If there are many people today who don't exercise self-control, is it because they think there are no dangers? Is it because they don't want to survive? Is it because they think they have nothing to lose?—or nothing to gain? There is a last question that suggests itself about those who never scan the skies, who never dream of danger, who disbelieve in the poison they have been taking for years: Are they alive? Or are they dead? But that is a question that only God (and, perhaps, they themselves) can answer. Who had the inspired writer in mind when he wrote: " I know your works; you have the name of being alive, and you are dead. . . . Remember then what you have received and heard; keep that, and repent. If you will not awake, I will come like a thief, and you will not know at what hour I will come upon you."[7]

Parents' hearts

Not to be scared about one's own survival; how crazy! Not to be scared about one's children survival; how thoughtless, or how criminal and inhuman! And that brings us back to the tremendous spectacle of so many parents nowadays who seem to contemplate, in all indifference, the exploitation and destruction of their children's lives, and who at times even contribute to their destruction by their own self-deception, by their practice of "double-standard" morality, by their selfishness and weakness in not denying themselves what they should not want their children to read or see.

Has the love of such parents for their children completely died? I do not think so. I think it has simply gone (or been put) to sleep. It can therefore be awakened. But when will that awakening come?

In this context there often comes to my mind a phrase in which St Luke describes the future mission of John the Baptist as Precursor of Christ. He says he will "turn the hearts of parents towards their children."[8] Could it not be that this is the problem today: that parents do not love their children enough; that their hearts are not sufficiently turned towards them? A conversion of their parents' hearts is what the world's young people need.

If parents really turn their hearts towards their children, they will have no trouble in seeing how they should try to be a model for them. They will see the need to be sincere and demanding with themselves, practising self-control, refusing to let themselves see or read many things that attract them, in the conviction that this fortitude of theirs is a source of strength for their children, and that they are giving them an example of real human maturity and of christian living—an example that they can respect and imitate.

If parents really turn their hearts towards their children, they will no longer remain blind to the criminal exploitation of which they are being made the main object. And with the awakening of parental love, there will come an arousal of

145

public opinion, an upsurge of moral indignation and—at last—a genuine, popular, massive pressure on the public authorities to remedy the abuses of the present situation.

The abuses of censorship?

State control is not enough to stop the moral decay of our world. Only self-control can to do that. But State control is also necessary, for there will always be some people who are not prepared to exercise self-control. There will always be some unscrupulous persons who are bent on making a name or a fortune for themselves, through sexual exploitation. And these people need to be restrained.

If, as we indicated, there is a public right to clean streets and unpolluted air, and a corresponding obligation on the part of the public authorities to restrain those who cause physical contamination, there are equal rights and duties in regard to moral contamination.

So, unless one wishes to be a party to the exploitation of the young (and the not so young) and the general corruption of society, there is no alternative but to support and demand some form of responsible public censorship. We will be more convinced and more convincing in our demands if we learn to see through the smoke-screen of anti-censorship propaganda so effectively raised today. . . .

Censorship, it is commonly said, is subject to manipulation, political control, abuse. . . . No doubt. But—as we have amply suggested—so is freedom. I may agree with the person who cries "Freedom is better than censorship", provided he agrees with me that the *abuses* of freedom are *worse* than the abuses of censorship. And the abuses of freedom are rampant and visible on all sides today, and do incalculable damage (in their personalities and humanity) to millions, while the abuses of censorship are infinitely less frequent and, above all, affect or damage (essentially in their pocketbooks) very few.

Besides, I just don't accept the contrast implied in the position: "Freedom—even if it involves some pornography—is better than censorship." Pornography *is* censorship, in as much as it means consciously and deliberately silencing and

146

suppressing other more human, more important and more noble aspects of sex than the merely animal and physical. A government therefore that does not face up to its responsibility to censor pornography is in fact censoring freedom, is threatening and limiting people's freedom to be masters of self, to avoid having an obsessed and inflamed imagination, to be able to respect themselves and others, to love and to be happy.

Governmental incompetence

Some governments today seem to have absolutely renounced their duty to regulate these matters. Their irresponsibility would, in certain cases, seem to be based on an ignorance of human nature such as to render them totally unfit and incompetent to govern.

What is one to make of the situation in certain countries where the government launches a massive campaign against cigarette smoking at the same time as it legalises abortion and passes ever more permissive sex laws? Does it not realise that a person's moral health—the very fibre of his character—will be much more certainly undermined by pornography than the health of his body can ever be by smoking?

It is true that the authorities in question just clapped a sort of super-tax on pornographic films and shows. But, one asks: is this so called "economic censure" seriously meant to be a restraining measure? Is it likely to stop the pornographic performances, or will it just mean that, to cover the sur-tax, the public will be asked to pay more to see these shows? What sort of government concern does this reveal? It is possible that we are reaching an acme of political irony: governments after all have hitherto generally claimed the right to send people to prison for not paying their taxes. Could it be that they are now going to send them to prison—to moral enslavement—for *paying* them!

Sex, a private matter?

Our Western governments may be sincere in their concern about their citizen's welfare. The trouble is that they just don't seem to know what this welfare involves and demands.

And surely nothing more disastrous can happen to a society than that the power to govern should be held by those who do not know what the object of government is?

The object of government is indeed to procure the public welfare or common good. But the common good is not achieved just because the Gross National Product or the per capita income are growing; or people enjoy good public health or postal services. The common good is being achieved when a government creates and defends conditions where men can live as men, and this means protecting whatever is favourable to human and personal dignity, and restraining those who would degrade or exploit others (whether economically, or—more importantly—morally).

Government responsibility has become restricted to the administration of things, and no longer covers the development of person. Politicians nowadays are practically all economic philosophers. They have an economic idea of man; they have no *human* idea of economics. And so they have no real human—man-centered—idea of the societies they have to govern.

Only a government without a true philosophy of man could yield to the apparently simple thesis (pushed by ingenuous liberals or not so ingenuous marxists) that sex is a private matter and one in which governments and laws have no right to interfere or attempt to regulate. . . .

The thesis is apparently simple. but it is also demonstrably false. For sex, as we have seen, is an area of human weakness—open therefore to unscrupulous exploitation—just as, when uncontrolled and especially when exploited, it is paradoxically a force making for violence and for the destruction of social peace. There are indeed private aspects to sex; but uncontrolled or exploited sex is not one of them.

Appendix: Abortion

What is abortion?

The answer to this question, until about twenty-five or thirty years ago, was very simple. Abortion meant killing an unborn child, killing a human being whose peculiar weakness consisted in its inability to survive outside its mother's womb. And there were two moral evaluations of this action:

1) that it was a *justifiable* homicide—in certain cases. This was the position of many non-Catholics, although not by any means of all;

2) that it was an *unjustifiable* homicide, i.e. that it was always murder, and therefore could never be licit. This was the Catholic position, shared by the Greek Orthodox Church and by many other religious and non-religious people.

The reasons behind the first position—justifiable homicide— were simple: that in the extreme case (the only one contemplated) of conflict between the *life* of the mother and the *life* of the child, the mother's life is more valuable, and the child's life should be sacrificed so that the mother can survive. The extreme case would be a pregnancy such that, if let come to term, the mother—and perhaps the child too—would die.

What is one to think of this position? Two things: a) one can easily accept that it was inspired by a sincere humanitarian feeling; b) that the principles on which it was based—that one human life is worth more than another, and that one can kill an innocent person in order to save another—opened the door inevitably to the position on abortion that is rapidly becoming generalized to-day: the position of those who campaign for abortion 'on demand', with no more justification than the fact that the mother—or perhaps the State—demands it.

As regards the Catholic position it is enough to say for the moment that it is based on the clear principle that every human being receives its life directly from God, and only God can take that life away, unless a person fortifies his right to life by a voluntary criminal aggression. It is not possible to imagine a more innocent person than an unborn child; therefore one cannot directly kill it for any cause whatsoever.

Such was the situation as regards abortion not very many years ago. An overall situation where it was easy to indicate and describe the points of agreement and the points of disagreement. There was agreement, between both sides, as to the nature of abortion: that it meant killing a child, that it was homicide, that the being in the mother's womb was a human being. And there was disagreement as to the licitness of this homicide: for some it was always illicit; for others it was, in certain grave cases, justifiable and licit. It is worth adding that even in the countries where this latter viewpoint prevailed and the civil law recognised the legality of abortion (in such extreme cases), the same legislation forbade and punished abortions performed in the absence of such exceptional cases or circumstances.

The position today

Now, if we examine the present-day situation, it so happens that to this question—what is abortion?—we find not two but three answers:

> 1) that is a non-justifiable homicide; i.e. the Catholic position, reaffirmed, be it noted, by Vatican Council II— in the strongest terms—which says (in the *Constitution on the Church in the Modern World*, 51) that abortion is an 'abominable crime';
> 2) that it is a justifiable homicide, in certain circumstances; i.e. the position—already commented on—of certain non-Catholics;
> 3) that it is *not a homicide at all!* This is the position with which I wish especially to deal, for it is generally the position of the modern "pro-choice" campaigners, and it is the ideological position—the new 'moral' basis—by which they seek to justify what cannot be justified.

150

Reformulating the problem

Abortion, say the new liberal reformers, is not a homicide at all, for a very simple reason: that what is killed is not a human being, that what is in the uterus *is not human*.

It is obvious that this supposition means a complete reformulation of the abortion problem. The reformulation is in fact so complete that if the supposition on which it is based is accepted, the problem aspect of abortion practically disappears for many people, and abortion becomes a matter—so they suggest—almost devoid of any difficulties of a moral nature.

Why the reformulation?

Perhaps the first thing to do in relation to this new position is to ask why and how it should have arisen in such a few years. It is not difficult to find the answer.

Everyone likes to feel humanitarian. The "liberals" of today's moral positivist school like not only to feel humanitarian but also to be able to proclaim themselves such.

The liberal humanitarian sense of non-Catholics of thirty years ago found no excessive difficulty in accepting that the life of an unborn child should be sacrificed to save the life of a mother. The years have passed and, with the years, two main factors have intervened. One is that advances in medicine have practically eliminated the extreme case of *either* the mother's life *or* the child's. Despite this—and here is the second factor—the demand for abortions has increased. There are many motives behind this increase. They include some "indications" of a more or less medical nature: the mother's poor health, the strain which a pregnancy represents on her nerves, etc. The main motive, however, is simply the growing birth-control mentality. Despite their being wrapped up in apparently disinterested references to world population problems, the motives for abortion in one individual case after another—at least in the more developed countries—can almost always be reduced to an *inability to look on the child with love*. It is, after all, an incapacity to love which makes a couple think of their unborn baby as no more than a burden: the burden of the pregnancy and of the care it will require after. It is an incapacity to love which makes a family dwell

151

on the fact that, if the child is born, they will have to give up some material comfort. It is an incapacity to love which makes a mother not want to bear and give birth to the child she has conceived.

Turning the fetus into a 'thing'

To kill a child in order to save the *life* of a mother was not repugnant to the humanitarian sense of some liberals of thirty years ago. To *kill a child* in order to save the *convenience* of the mother—her reluctance to go through with an existing pregnancy—or to save the *well being* of the other children or the *financial position* of the family: to accept this is to ask a lot of the humanitarian sense of anyone, however liberal he or she may be.

The solution has been found quite simply. So it is too much to sacrifice a child's life for the sake of a mother's caprice, or a family's standard of living, or a society's welfare? . . . Then let it not be the life of a child which is sacrificed; let it be no more than the life of a fetus. Let us conclude, moreover (according to someone's happy theory), that the fetus is not human (let us conclude it, I say, because we certainly cannot prove it), and what we are left with, after all that, is neither homicide nor infanticide, but only only feticide—which (let us be persuaded) is no more significant in the moral order than the killing of some microbes (also foreign and unwanted bodies) by means of an injection of penicillin.

Here is the new moral view of the abortion question. We are going to have to face the objection (so they would seem to have reasoned) that abortion is homicide; and certainly, at least in the new cases we are interested in, it would be difficult to justify a homicide . . . Let us not waste time trying to justify it. Let us say, in all simplicity, that it is not a homicide, because what is aborted has not a human nature; it is therefore not a member of our human race, it is a *thing*. And since things possess no rights, the problem quite disappears.

Two-stage abortion

What this view offers us is, so to speak, a two-stage abortion: a physical operation preceded by a metaphysical operation, a physical abortion with a metaphysical pre-requisite: that of suppressing the human *identity* of the living being in the womb. Once this metaphysical operation has been performed (a truly painless operation—provided one applies a little anaesthesia to one's conscience . . .), the surgical or pharmacological operation necessary to suppress what "remains" in the uterus offers no special difficulty, since this "remainder"— duly disenfranchised from among the race of men and deprived of its human status and rights,—is no longer a human being, it is no more than a non-human thing.

Let us grasp this clearly. The essential argument of the modern abortionists is not (except in two cases which we will examine later on) that new indications or reasons for abortion have been discovered, new reasons of note which were hitherto unknown. Their argument is different and it is important, I repeat, to grasp it. They are not mainly saying that there are more reasons than those formerly known, in order to kill what is in the womb. They are saying that what is in the womb has less importance than what was formerly believed; it has less value. It has no human value and possesses no human rights.

The Catholic argument

The whole of the Catholic argument—and I would maintain that from whatever angle one may consider the matter, it is the only truly rational, truly scientific and truly humanitarian argument—is that the unborn child is already a human being, and enjoys all the natural rights of every human being, among which the main right is the right to life; and moreover, that its particular situation as a *defenceless* human being confers on it the right to special protection from the civil law.

It is interesting to recall that the United Nations, in plenary session in November 1959, unanimously approved a declaration of the rights of the child in the following terms: "the child, in virtue of its lack of physical and intellectual maturity needs special protection and care, including adequate legal

153

protection, both *before* and after birth." This declaration was renewed later on in the International Human Rights Conference, in Teheran, in May 1968.

Embryology gives supporting evidence

From the theological viewpoint, specifically human life begins with the infusion, by God, of the soul into the new embryonic organism. Although there has been no dogmatic declaration on this point, the Magisterium of the Church has crystallized in the clear teaching that the beginning of this personal human life should be computed from the moment of conception: the moment in which the ovum has been fertilized.[1] This teaching is reflected in the relation between certain liturgical feasts—the Annunciation (March 25th) and Christmas; the Immaculate Conception and the Feast of the Nativity of Our Lady (September 8th)—and is supported by the dispositions of Canon Law (vid. canon 71). Much more significant and interesting is the fact that this universal teaching of the Church is supported and fully borne out by all the scientific advances in modern embryology. So true is this that one can affirm that, *from a scientific viewpoint, the truth of the catholic teaching on this point has been placed beyond all doubt*. Modern embryological research has shown that the human being, organically speaking, is fully constituted by the fertilisation of the ovum, and that everything that follows is simply the process of development of an already existing human organism without it being possible to indicate any subsequent datum or fact on which one could reasonably base the supposed beginning of a personal human life.

The arbitrariness of the abortionist position

It is significant that abortionists or pro-choice people never speak of an unborn *child*. They rigorously use the term "embryo" of "fetus". If they are asked (a question which is not much to their liking) to define what is a fetus, they define it as "potential human life", speaking of it on occasion even as "potential life". And if they are obliged to pursue their pseudo-philosophical or pseudo-juridical line, they maintain that this potential life does not become real and actual human life—with its corresponding rights—until birth, or at least until the fetus is viable. This evidently is pure arbitrariness. It is impossible to advance any rational or scientific principle or fact on which it can be based. It is simply the product of prejudice. Is anyone prepared seriously to maintain that what is born to-day is human, but that what was in the womb yesterday was not? If one tries to make an argument out of viability, can one say that a new born child is significantly more viable than a child still in its mother's womb? If anything, it is definitely less viable. One has to put more care, and not less, in feeding it. One has to take greater precautions to make sure, for example, that it does not fall down the stairs, precautions that its mother guaranteed it far more effectively when it was still in the womb.

If human personality and human rights are not acquired until one is really viable, until one can get by and survive by oneself, it is doubtful that any child less than six or seven years old is really a human being.

I repeat: all the scientific arguments are against the position of the abortionists and in favour of the Catholic position. If someone wants a practical test of this, then let him simply ask a non-Catholic doctor who has performed an abortion whether what he has extracted from the womb is no more than a thing; or whether it is a living being. And if it is a living being, of what species is it? No; the abortionist position is not based on science or on reason; it is based on prejudices and interests, neither of which have anything very humanitarian about them.

The woman who aborts . . .

As a priest I have learned to distinguish between the sin and the sinner. I have also learned that although one can and at times one must judge actions and facts, it is difficult and risky to judge persons. Only God can do that properly. In a moment of temptation, a pregnant woman—who does not want to have her child and decides to abort—can have been swayed by countless factors: factors of personal formation, of the influences coming from her environment, her relatives or friends, factors of loneliness, of fear, of nervous strain. . . . We

155

cannot judge the degree of blame which may rest on a woman in such a situation. Only God, I repeat, who takes everything into account, can judge this. We can however judge something else, or at least form a reliable opinion about it, i.e. what will become of this woman, in human terms, according as she repents or not of what she has done.

Let us not fool ourselves. The woman who has procured an abortion knows that she has procured the death, the murder, of her own child, the fruit of her own womb. And she remains with a deep wound in her conscience. A permissive society may find no difficulty in forgiving her. The worst of it is that she will not be able to forgive herself, or to forget. And my experience is that in the exceptional cases where a woman does succeed in silencing her conscience, she does so at the cost of moral suicide: she destroys her very conscience and her sense of values, she de-feminizes and de-humanizes herself. Her maternal instinct in particular, and her whole capacity of loving, suffer enormous and irreparable damage.

The Church never wants to condemn persons. If it condemns sin, if it condemns wrong actions, it is in order to help people have clear ideas, to help them look into their conscience (which, if they have done wrong, will also accuse them) so that, *by repenting*, they can find pardon and peace. It is those that condone immoral actions who may be condemning a person to a terrible life of mental anguish.

Personalization and depersonalization

This leads us to touch on another pseudo-argument of the abortionists, according to which the determination that the unborn child is a person should depend not on biological facts, nor even on time-factors (viability or birth), but on a psychological factor. Playing with concepts drawn from modern psychology—concepts that emphasize the importance of intersubjective relationships in the process of "personalization"—some abortionists have suggested that the unborn child cannot properly be regarded as a person before it has been *accepted* by its parents; if this acceptance is lacking—so the argument runs—it cannot be considered a person nor does it possess personal rights.

This argument runs into the same sort of trouble as the "viability" argument. It "proves" too much. On its basis a one year old child or a five year old would not be a person either, if its parents have not "accepted" it. Obviously it is *before*, and not after, begetting a child that the parents have to decided if they want it or not. Before, it was a possibility, precisely no more than a "potentiality". After, it is a reality, and that reality is a person just as much as the one day old or the one month old baby. It is a person who therefore possesses its personality, in the fullest human sense, a personality that makes it the subject of rights.[2]

There is, of course, an ambiguity in the personalization argument. But it is an ambiguity which, when brought to light, rebounds back against the very proponents of the argument. Evidently, if one asks whether the unborn child has its own "personality" in the *popular* sense—in the sense of possessing a whole personal manner of being: of thinking and speaking and acting—the answer is No. In this sense the unborn child is not "personalized", nor is the one day old, nor the one month old, child; just as, in this same sense, the three year old, or the five year old child, is only very slightly personalized.

Since "personalization" really means the process of the *development* of one's individual personality, this is evidently a process that takes years: all the year's of one's life, in fact. Only with the years—with all that the years bring in terms of human experience: of generosity or selfishness, of virtues and sins, of learning to respect and love others or of failing to learn to love, of having faced up to just responsibilities or of having rejected them—does a person develop his or her distinctive personality.

Self-realization for "liberated" women?

The personalization argument—which has no application to the case of the unborn child (what personality can be *developed* by a person who is killed?)—does however apply very clearly precisely to the case of the mother who aborts. For here one can ask, and largely foresee, "What sort of personality is going to be developed by a *person who kills?*"

Modern psychology insists that men and women "realize" or "fulfil" themselves above all in their relations with other people, and that one of the clearest proofs of the presence or absence of personality is the capacity or incapacity for establishing interpersonal relationships.

What personality is going to be developed by a woman who, before the most intimate inter-personal relationship imaginable—the relationship between her own person and the person of the child she has conceived; the (truly unique) relationship between her own body and the body of the child in her womb—, rejects and destroys that relationship, killing her child and having its body consigned to a hospital incinerator?

Through what type of later relationships will a woman be able to "realize" herself if her reaction to this sacred mother-child relationship has been to extirpate her most intimate instincts of motherhood and pity from her heart, by extirpating her child from her body?

It is sad to see pro-choice propaganda present abortion as a "right" of every woman, claiming this right precisely in the name of women's "liberation". It is sad propaganda that can only turn the women who use this "right", into sad and embittered women. Who is going to *liberate* them afterwards from the awareness of what, in violation of their most intimate human instincts, they have done?

Some years ago, when the proposal to "liberalize" the abortion law in England was being debated, I recall seeing a television programme which included interviews with a series of women who had each had a number of abortions. The interviewers's questions were evidently aimed at "proving" one point: that neither physically or psychologically had they suffered any adverse effects from the abortions. What the women *said*, in answer, corroborated the thesis fully. However, I still retain a vivid memory of their hardened faces, their way of answering, their evident concern to justify themselves, their insistence that they had never been troubled by the least feeling of repugnance or remorse, their air of proud and sad loneliness; in a word, the impression of what I have mentioned earlier: a brutal defeminization and dehumanization.

I would now like to examine two points: two new "indications" or arguments that tend to make ever more frequent appearances in the pro-abortion campaign. I will consider them briefly, not because these arguments are less important—they are terribly significant and important—but simply because space does not permit any more extensive treatment.

The "eugenic" argument

The first argument is that of the so-called "eugenic" indication; in other words, the probability or possibility that the already conceived child may be born with some physical or mental defect. All modern abortion law reform includes a clause legalizing an abortion carried out for eugenic reasons. The clause containing the eugenic indication tends to be very short, and many people probably look on it as one indication more, more or less of the same order as the others.

It is no such thing! If the philosophy of life that underlies the other indications is repellent, the ideology underlying this clause is of an infinitely worse order. Let us state it very clearly: this indication is the fruit of no mere selfish hedonism; nor is it the product of an individualistic materialism that has lost its sense of direction and values. . . . By means of this little clause, a clear, powerful and repugnant philosophy is opening a way for itself—a legal way—into our western countries. The philosophy, or rather ideology, of this clause is that of racial purity and has little or no essential difference from the hitlerian ideology. For eugenicism, after all, simply means this: we don't want any inferior stock, we don't want any "sub-standard" specimens who could disturb the tranquil contemplation of our Brave New World, demanding compassion, appealing for charity or affection, or simply reminding us that there is a God to whom we ought to be grateful for the good things we enjoy.

Lives not worth living

Let us not forget what this clause means in practice. It means, each time it is applied, that one or several persons are making

159

the following judgment: "In our opinion, this life"—and they are speaking of another human being already in existence—"this life is not worth living. It is (or rather, it may later turn out to be) so defective that it is better for it to die now."

This criticism, it should be noted, is valid even for those who maintain that the fetus is *not yet* a human person. They are making the same judgment: "This life, which—unless we kill it—will develop into a human person, will develop into a human life unworthy of being lived. Therefore, let us kill it."

The essential and only basis to what we call democratic rights is that every being is an inviolable value; and that no one—no State, no authority, no person—can decide that any one else's life is useless and *dispensable*.

One can make the judgment that someone is living in conditions unworthy of a human being, and then make every effort to remedy those conditions. That is humanitarian.

What one cannot do—in the name of humanitarianism—is to make the judgment that someone is not worthy to live—*even if he may have to live in conditions unworthy of a human being*. That is not a humanitarian, but a totalitarian judgment. When one makes that judgment one has put an end to humanitarianism.

Consequences of eugenicism

The eugenic arguments is subject to many further criticisms. I will limit myself to two:

a) The prognosis that the child may possibly be born defective cannot be made with absolute certainty. If abortions are performed on this ground, the result will be that in a high percentage of the cases (some estimates say that it could be as high as 50%) quite normal children will be killed. It would be much more logical, from the eugenicist viewpoint (and if the eugenicists consider themselves humanitarian, it would also be, for them, much more humanitarian) to let all these pregnancies come to term and once the children have been born, kill those who in fact prove defective. If anyone says that this would be too repugnant, I could not agree more; but it is the logic of eugenicism that is repugnant.

160

b) If, in virtue of the principle that defective lives are not worth living, it is humane to kill in order to prevent a person being born who *may* turn out to be defective, it is unquestionably more humane still to kill a person who has *already* turned out to be defective, to kill a defective person already born, whether one day old or one year, or twenty or forty or sixty. And that person can be killed because (it is a point inherent in the same principle) he is not possessed of human life by a sufficiently good title. His physical or mental defect has made his very *right to life* defective. He can be killed not perhaps for the "defect" of being a Jew, but for that of being crazy or disabled or chronically ill or simply aged.

The acceptance of eugenicist abortion means—*whether the public at large is aware of the fact or not*—the acceptance not only of the principles underlying euthanasia, but of all of the principles of the politics of racial purity: the policy of the elimination of the unfit, of those unworthy of life, of those who do not measure up to the quality standards laid down—by the controllers that be—for the human stock. . . .

But surely—I hear the objection—all of this is rather exaggerated? No. It is not exaggeration. It is simply a *projection*. It is simply to follow out the logical consequences of the new abortionist philosophies, and to project them on to the practical life of a perhaps not very far-off future.

To-morrow's world will be the product of the tendencies and ideologies that have prevailed in the world of today. What will that world be like? It is something to think about, while there is still time to think. This is not the moment to play the ostrich, burying our heads in the sand. It is an elementary responsibility to read the signs of the times, to see where a large part of our modern civilization is heading and to ask ourselves if we too want to go in that direction. To prefer not to ask oneself the question, is the surest way of finding oneself eventually dragged in that very direction.

Excommunicating oneself from humanity . . .

Let me therefore re-emphasize what I have said earlier. Abortion— tolerated or legalized; looked on with indifference or with approval—represents an extreme of barbarity that is hard to surpass. One could well see in it a symbol of how our civilization seems bent on destroying the very seeds of survival that it bears within itself.

It is understandable that the Church should wish to emphasize the gravity of this "abominable crime", by decreeing an *ipso facto* excommunication not only for the woman who procures an abortion, but also for all who have effectively intervened in the abortion, even though this has been no more than by simply advising it (Code of Canon Law; canon 1398 and canon 1329).

An abortionist—again I am thinking above all of those who try to justify this crime—excommunicates himself from the most elementary human community, the community of those who strive to respect the human rights of others, whatever their religion, race, colour, social position, state of physical or mental health, or age.

The demographic argument

The second new argument which is used to support abortion is the demographic argument. There are already countries where abortion is imposed as a means of demographic control. Elsewhere, for the moment, the matter rather works the other way round; i.e. the constant propaganda about over-population acts as a factor in favour of abortion. As public opinion is "mentalized" so as to think that it is not quite right to have more than one or two children, that one ought not to have more than one or two, that this is an urgent and imperative duty, that its non-observance must be regarded, initially, as a total lack of responsibility and, next, as a flagrant crime against society. . . . then it becomes progressively easier to persuade the public that abortion is not a crime at all; that, far from being a crime, it may be the best and most appropriate means to get people to fulfill a strict duty.

It is logical that those to whom this "argument" appeals should be attracted also by the fact that abortion is, without the slightest doubt, the most effect means to check population growth. It requires no exceptional degree of intelligence to realize that the best means to ensure that there is no excess population is to kill the "surplus". This, in all its true crudeness, is the way of thinking of some people, although they do not—as yet—dare to present it quite so bluntly. But it is as blunt as that; so much so that one could well ask those who think this way to explain if there is any real difference, as a means to their end, between the scalpel and the machine-gun.

Introduction

1.   As is well known, the first significant change in the Protestant judgment on contraception was at the Lambeth Conference of 1929.

2.   Pope John Paul II, *Familiaris Consortio,*11.

Chapter 1 : Marriage in Crisis?

1.   Vatican II, *Constitution on the Church in the World of Today*, 50.

2.   "Man cannot attain that true happiness for which he yearns with all the strength of his spirit, unless he keeps the laws which the Most High God has engraved in his very nature. These laws must be wisely and lovingly observed." Pope Paul VI, Enc. *Humanae Vitae*, 31.

3.   Matt 19, 6.

4.   Gen 1, 28.

5.   *Constitution on the Church in the World of Today*, 48.

6.   Josemaría Escrivá de Balaguer, *Conversations* (Shannon, 1972), 94.

7.   *Constitution on the Church in the World of Today*, 48.

8.   Cf. *Humanae Vitae*, 8.

9.   Cf. *Humanae Vitae*, 9.

10.   Jacques Leclercq, *Le Mariage Chrétien*, ch. 6.

11.   *Ibid.*

12.   Cf. *Humanae Vitae*, 9.

13.   Leclercq, *op. cit.*, ch. 5.

Chapter 2 : Married love and contraception

1.   We are obviously not speaking here of the gift of self which a person may make to God.

2.   Seed is here intended to refer equally to the male or the female generative element.

3.   In this way in fact the uniqueness of the decision to marry a particular person is reaffirmed in each marital act. By every single act of true intercourse, each spouse in *confirmed* in the unique status of being husband or wife to the other.

4.   The "language of the body" is of course a key expression in Pope John Paul II's writings on sexuality and marriage.

5. "Contraception contradicts the *truth* of conjugal love,' Pope John Paul II, Address, 17 September 1983.

6. This still remains true even in cases where, for some reason or another, the spouses cannot have children. Their union in such cases, just as their union during the wife's pregnancy, draws its deepest meaning from the fact that both their conjugal act and the intention behind it are "open to life" even though no life can actually result from the act. It is their basic openness to life which gives the act its meaning and dignity. Just as the absence of this openness is what undermines the dignity and meaning of the act when the spouses, without serious reasons, deliberately limit their marital intercourse to the infertile periods.

7. Obviously we are not referring here to those occasions in which, out of justice to a third party, one of the spouses is under an *obligation* to observe some secret, e.g., of a professional nature. Fulfillment of such an obligation is in no way a violation of the rights of married intimacy.

8. If it is not sexuality that each spouse in contraceptive intercourse gives to or takes from the other, what does each one in fact actually take or give? In what might be termed the better cases, it is a form of love—divorced from sexuality. In other cases, it is merely pleasure, also—be it noted—divorced from sexuality. In one case or the other, contraceptive spouses always deny themselves sexuality. Their marriage, deprived of a true sexual relationship, suffers in consequence.

9. General Audience, 21 November 1979.

Chapter 3 : Children as values

1. I know an African family with eighteen children and no car, and an American "family" (if it can be called that) with eighteen cars and no children. And I honestly think that the African family is much happier: about eighteen times as much.

2. *Familiaris Consortio*, 20.

3. Is 43, 1.

4. Pope John Paul II, General Audience, 28 April 1982.

5. Cf. Gen 4, 1.

6. The love of naturally barren couples, to whom God does not give children, should of course also grow; but it too needs dedication to others, if it is to do so.

7. By one or two children perhaps; or perhaps by five or six. It is only God who knows the measure of support each marriage requires. Hence the vital need for spouses, if they are to resolve the matter successfully and happily, to approach it prayerfully.

8. Homily, 7 October 1979.

9. *Constitution on the Church in the World of Today*, 50

10. Cf. *On the Scope and Nature of University Education*, Discourse IV.

11. Deut 30, 19.

12. There was a Babe born once in Bethlehem and nothing was or is better than that Babe, who shares his goodness with each baby born, and would have wished to share it with many who have not been and never will be born.

13. Cf. *Humanae Vitae*, 21.

14. An African footnote. Disconcerted by Planned Parenthood arguments, a Kenyan remarked: "Traditionally if the neighbours' cow gave birth to a calf, one congratulated the family, because their standard of life had increased. Nowadays if the wife gives birth to a child, one is apparently supposed to sympathize with them, because their standard of life has gone down. . . . I have to figure that one out."

15. *Humanae Vitae*, 10.

Chapter 4 : Divorce: husband and wife

1. Cf. Matt 19, 8–9.

2. Cf. Council of Trent, Session 24, can. 5; Vatican Council II, *Constitution on the Church in the World of Today*, 48-50.

3. *Collier's Encyclopedia*, Vol. 8, p. 281 (1968 Edition).

4. National Center for Health Statistics, Washington, DC.

5. See Chapter One.

6. In fact, if two people got on "happily" in marriage, without ever having had to make any real effort at it, their marriage—however "happy" (and it would, I think, be a mediocre happiness)—would not have been a *successful* marriage: for it would not have succeeded in maturing them as persons.

7. Even to love God, Who has no defects, is hard; because although He has no defects, *we* have. Each one of us finds it difficult to come out of self and to give ourself to another—which is what love implies. We find that difficult even when the Other is perfect. When the other is not perfect, as occurs in all purely human relations—marriage included—, it is harder still.

8. See Acts 20, 35.

9. If it were human nature always to "feel in love", then there would be no need for a law of indissolubility. . . . In this sense, it is precisely for those who no longer *feel* in love that the law is meant! . . .

10. *Newsweek*, 13 February 1967.

Chapter 5 : Divorce: the children

1. Matt 19, 6.
2. This idea—that a new marriage will enable the children to refind a father or a mother's love—far from being an argument in favor of divorce, points up one of the worst effects of remarriage. It may well be, for instance, that their mother no longer loves their father, and feels she loves another man instead. But only an extreme of selfishness or of psychological blindness can lead her to think that her children can—or should—make such an easy transfer of natural and deeply rooted affections. The mere wish—let alone the attempt—to get them to transfer their filial love to a substitute parent, thereby rejecting their real father or mother, can produce most serious psychological consequences.
3. Therefore couples who *deliberately* remain childless, so that they can enjoy each other's love more, are leaving that love defenseless against the inevitable onset of selfishness.

Chapter 6 : Parents, children and the rules of life

1. Cf. 1 Tim 2,4.
2. J. Escrivá, *Christ is Passing By* (Dublin, 1985), 114.
3. Perhaps no one has ever insisted as much as Msgr Josemaria Escrivá on the inseparable harmony that should exist between "individual freedom and the personal responsibility that must always go with it" (*Christ is Passing By*, 184; cf. *Conversations with Msgr Escrivá, op. cit*, 100).
4. *Conversations*, 100.
5. See also pp. 143 ff.
6. *Christ is Passing By*, 28.

Chapter 7 : Ideals in youth

1. If the passage of the years is not to undermine married happiness, each of the partners needs to keep on seeing some ideal aspect in the other. Yet it is obvious that no man, and no woman, can remain indefinitely the ideal person for the other. He or she has too many defects, and these defects are inevitably going to be discovered. Nevertheless, even though it is inevitable that the partners in marriage discover each other's defects, this should not necessarily lead to the collapse of ideal love for them. It will have a moderating effect on it, in the sense that they should come to realize that only God is perfect. But, defects and all, husband or wife should continue

to be the ideal for their partner. The real danger comes from pride. Pride tends to blind us to our own defects, and to make us much too sharp-sighted as to the defects of others. Similarly it makes us more aware of our own virtues, and blinds us to the virtues of others. If husband and wife are to keep up their ideal love for one another, if they are to love each other more and more as time passes, then they need, with God's grace, to learn to be humble. Humility will make each one more aware of his or her own defects than of those of their partner. At the same time it will make them regard their partner's virtues or good points as greater and more important than any they themselves may possess. This is the only way that each of them can remain convinced that they are enjoying a love of which they are not worthy. The ideal they were looking for in their marriage will remain standing.

2. *Journal*, III, 214-215.

3. And how about the lives of the saints, both men and women? Terrific reading, certainly, for pre-adolescents—up to perhaps 11 to 12 years old. If after that it is more difficult to find lives of saints capable of capturing the interest and enthusiasm of adolescents, the fault must be laid at the door not of the saints but of their biographers. Most of these move around in a sort of dis-incarnated supernatural world and seem to be incapable of pointing up the *natural* virtues and the humanly attractive and moving aspects of these heroes. But there are signs that things are improving in this area.

4. Cf. J. Escrivá, *The Way* (Dublin 1985), 88.

5. *Marialis Cultus*, 47.

6. Rom 1, 6.

7. Mk 8, 38.

8. Jn 8, 32.

9. Jn 13, 35

10. Matt 20, 28.

11. *The Way, op. cit.*, 335.

Chapter 8 : The family and the permissive society

1. Even within marriage its use—if it is to remain noble and at the service of love—requires control and restraint. Where that restraint is lacking, sex, far from serving or fostering love, tends to destroy it; for it turns into an expression of selfishness.

2. Cf. Lk 18, 9.

3. Of course some will reject the concept of sex-addiction, or the idea that it corrupts or enslaves. This is like the drug-addict or alcoholic who says he is not addicted; that he just likes drink or drugs. I

would not argue with him. What he needs is help. But if he won't acknowledge his need he won't let himself be helped. Alcoholics Anonymous have spelled out this truth of life very clearly.

Others would even say that if people *prefer* pornography, they are not really being exploited: they are getting what they choose. Certainly; but what they choose is exploitation, even if, perhaps, they don't realise it. A large part of the exploitation lies precisely in manipulating the exploited into the idea that they are choosing freedom when in fact they are choosing slavery. Once the pornographer puts up signs outside his establishment saying "Slave shop"; "We offer slavery: attractive, indeed captivating, but slavery", then, though we may still call him an exploiter, we will no longer have to call him a hypocrite. In the same way as marxists must be called hypocrites for so long as they continue to manipulate the term "democracy". Can anything less democratic be imagined than marxist philosophy or tactics, or than a Communist state? We should therefore keep calling marxists hypocrites until they stop calling themselves democrats. Once the marxists cease to talk about democracy and say clearly: "What we offer is an earthly paradise where men will be born, reared, fed, put to work, made socially useful, and eventually hygienically buried and entirely forgotten, under the dictatorial control of a one-party State, where each one will be treated at all times as a strict economic unit and nothing more, where elementary material needs will be cared for, but where not the least vestige of personal or political freedom will remain . . .", when the Communists say this, then *we* will continue to say that their programmes are as mistaken and as hollow as ever, but we will no longer have to say that *they* are insincere. So with the pornographers.

One stage worse than the blind leading the blind, is the blind fooling the blind: the blind *blinding* the blind . . . The fact is that no one is qualified to speak about sex unless he acknowledges its *contradictions*: its noble function, if integrated into God's plans; but also its potential, if uncontrolled or exploited, for making slaves. Writers, artists, film producers, magazine editors, advertisers, today realise this potential and the profit it brings them. The problem is that their public often refuses to acknowledge it.

4.   And, since God's will is that we should be happy (his will is our happiness), if we do contravene it, we will not be happy.

5.   Cf pp. 138 f.

6.   After all, if a man is not in control of himself, he can be pretty sure that he is being controlled by someone else. This control or *manipulation* of the many by the few, especially through the medium

of sex, covers much wider fields and interests than might be at first imagined. We have spoken of the commercial pornographer who peddles pornography, and of his interest in breaking down the sales resistance of his potential clients. Let us not think, however, that he is the only one with a clear interest in promoting pornography. There have been recent developments in the commercial world in general which are significant. The use of a certain element of sex appeal in ordinary advertising has been a normal matter to which no one has ever dreamed of objecting. Pretty faces smilingly decorated ads for stage-coach trips in the last century and smilingly decorate ads for air-lines trips in this. Over the past years, however, this has degenerated in many cases into progressive and downright pornography. Why? If the degeneration is due to thoughtlessness on the part of the firms concerned (their simply letting themselves unwittingly be used by elements within the advertising profession), their witlessness is truly appalling. The possibility remains that it is due to deliberate policy; that certain manufacturers realise that it is easier to sell (anything) to people without self-control, and so they favour whatever breaks down that control. It is not a pleasant possibility. One cannot easily exclude the same unpleasant possibility from the sphere of politics. When one looks at certain political programmes which favour liberalization of censorship laws, etc., one wonders if the master thought in the mind of the "liberal" politicians who sponsor these policies could not be that they have a double manipulatory effect: they are vote-catching (people easily fall for the promise of easy freedom) and (so at least some people believe) they make for an enervated and therefore easily governed population. Some liberal politicians are well aware (even if their voters are not) that the permissive societies they are brain-childing are becoming more and more like Huxley's planned and totally manipulated *Brave New World*.They have even outdone Huxley's World Controllers in maintaining the fiction of freedom. The fact that they are wrong about such a liberalised society being more easily controllable (at least by democratic means); the fact that such societies inevitably lead to growing social violence and anarchy, and that in the end they can only be governed by sheer police force, merely underlines the ultimate purpose of these policies calculated, as they are, to destroy the very humanity of people's lives.

7. Rev 3, 1-3.
8. Lk 1, 17.

Appendix

1.   Some medieval theologians took the scholastic philosophical principle that the soul is the "substantial form" of the body, as basis for a theory of "retarded animation", according to which the fetus has at first no more than an animal or vegetable soul, and that a rational and human soul is infused only when it is sufficiently developed and can represent an adequate "receptacle" for this substantial form. With such a theory, it was impossible to assign other than a quite arbitrary moment for "animation"—which is what some scholastics in fact did (40- or 80-days after conception). Modern embryology has helped in the rejection of this theory and in the return to the earlier position (held, for instance, by Fathers of the Church such as St Basil or St Gregory) that the rational soul is present from the moment of conception. As can be seen, philosophy owes a debt to physiology in reaching a scientific understanding of the stage at which the human organism in fundamentally constituted, i.e. the basis stage of fertilization, at which therefore it can receive its "substantial form".

2.   We might note here that to the arguments given earlier, taken from embryology, we can add an argument taken from juridical science. All ancient and modern jurisprudences attribute to the unborn child full juridical personality expressed, for example, in its capacity to inherit or be the beneficiary of a will.